This book will fill you with compassion as you recognize God as your protector and provider. Your faith will be renewed and your worship will be transformed to honor Him as your Father. As you read these pages, God will smile upon you and hold you tenderly as you experience healing and victory through a lifestyle of worship. The author lays it in a powerful and profound way, sharing her personal experiences and how the glory of God delivered on every occasion. She addresses the subject of worship with great wisdom, compassion, and revelation. Read it, receive it, and rejoice in it on your way to divine destiny. You will surely survive every struggle and become an overcomer!

—Taiwo Kuku,
Senior Pastor, The Faith and Miracle Center

EXPECT THE UNEXPECTED

EXPECT THE UNEXPECTED

Experience Healing

and Total Victory

KAREN L. BRADWELL, PH.D

© 2009, 2013 by Dr. K.L. Bradwell. All rights reserved.
2nd Printing 2014

Trusted Books is an imprint of Deep River Books. The views expressed or implied in this work are those of the author. To learn more about Deep River Books, go online to www.DeepRiverBooks.com.

No part of this publication may be reproduced, stored in a retrieval system, or transmitted in any way by any means—electronic, mechanical, photocopy, recording, or otherwise—without the prior permission of the copyright holder, except as provided by USA copyright law.

This book or parts thereof may not be reproduced in any form without written permission of the publisher and copyright owner.

Unless otherwise noted, all Scriptures are taken from the *Holy Bible, New International Version®, NIV®*. Copyright © 1973, 1978, 1984 by Biblica, Inc.™ Used by permission of Zondervan. All rights reserved worldwide. www.zondervan.com

ISBN 13: 978-1-63269-072-2
Library of Congress Catalog Card Number: 2009901931

To you, my Jesus, the Lover of my soul, the love of my life. You have taught my soul to sing, my heart to obey, and my spirit to soar. In worship and prayer, I have found in You a resting place of strength, power, and victory through many adversities.

To my family and inheritance. Thank you for your loyalty, steadfast love, and encouragement. You are most appreciated and I love you with all my heart.

To all my spiritual mothers, fathers, friends, and extended church family for your unconditional love, encouragement, guidance, and prayers.

CONTENTS

Foreword.................................. xi
Preface................................... xiii

Chapter One: Where Is My Daddy? 1
Chapter Two: Facing Life's Giants 19
Chapter Three: Strengthened in His Presence...33
Chapter Four: Keep on Moving and
    Don't Stop 47
Chapter Five: Worship Changes the
    Atmosphere...........................61
Chapter Six: Holy Ghost Power to Advance....73
Chapter Seven: The Setup for the Comeback...85

Chapter Eight: Healing and Restoration Are
    Yours 99
Chapter Nine: Setbacks Are Not Final 107
Chapter Ten: Enough Is Enough! 125

About the Author 141

FOREWORD

I READ WITH great interest as Dr. Bradwell lovingly and passionately developed her argument that "The presence of the Lord will always drive out the forces of darkness." Fully documented with both Scriptural verse and scholarly sources, as well as persuasively argued, this book has merit on several levels: as an inspirational piece that everyone can benefit from in their spiritual lives, as a record of Dr. Bradwell's own personal journey, and as a powerful document that beautifully explains God's love for us and His unfailing presence in our lives.

Every passage, every chapter, indeed every sentence, rings with the authority and majesty of the Truth itself: that the Word of God, enjoyed and deployed through devotional and sincere worship, can lead anyone and everyone to a new peace in their lives and, more importantly, to the promise of eternal salvation.

Although I am fairly well versed in these topics, I found myself learning new truths and rediscovering important knowledge I had not recalled for quite some time. Ultimately, Dr. Bradwell delivers a message that "Total deliverance, healing, divine restoration, and divine acceleration can be yours. Liberation from any kind of bondage, taskmaster, or oppression over our lives can be yours because of the Lord's Grace and favor." I applaud Dr. Bradwell for her excellent efforts and utmost wisdom in penning this inspirational for such a time as this.

—**Wald Carum**, PhD

PREFACE

"A Life of Prayer and Consecration
Is Preparation for a Dynamic Demonstration of
Kingdom Administration"

HAVE YOU EVER gone to a church service in search to find God or connect with Him? You find yourself at a dead end, roadblock in life carrying a deep inner turmoil only to find yourself disappointed. You pray, read the Holy Scriptures, join the choir, usher board, or some auxiliary. You gather a collection of self-help literature that overflows your library shelf. Sometimes you give a shout out to friends "let's get our party on tonight." So you party all night, take a shot of...and you find yourself doing things you would not "normally" do. At the end of the day, you look in the mirror and nothing has changed. There it is (your ugly situation) staring you right in the face, still searching, hurting, void, and empty. You release a heart cry "O God please help me."

No matter what has happened or the opposition, God is love and He delivers victory on every side. For in His presence there is fullness of miracles, supernatural manifestations of His provision, healing, restoration, and the power to overcome. In spite of where you've been, what you've done, or what has offended you, having a relationship with God through the thresholds of worship will transform your life, enable you to rise above every struggle, and empower you to advance through them all. "And now these three remain: faith, hope and love. But the greatest of these is love" (1 Corinthians 13:13). Coupled together these three are powerful ingredients that will create an atmosphere for the Almighty God to enter our arena. I call this atmosphere our life of *worship*. Worship to God is attributing one's love—one's loyalty, service, compassion, affection, worth, confidence, and appreciation—from his or her heart with unswerving faith, unswerving hope, and unswerving confidence that God is reliable and you can count on Him.

The world may expect you to become a product of the traumas and crisis. Society and sometimes those closest to you may label you as a failure and misfit; their expectation of your future states that you are hopeless, a "lost cause," and that you will never mount up to anything. You yourself may have embraced this lie as a truth and aimlessly you find

PREFACE

yourself wondering, living life unfulfilled, shallow, and empty. The Lord has a plan for you, a hope for you, and a future for you. And it's not what they expect. In the position of knowing the Father and communing with Him, you can expect the unexpected. Silver and gold have I none, but such as I have, I give You Jesus. Your past, your struggles, and your adversities will not determine your present, nor your future. There's a bright day ahead of you. Unexpected favor is before you. Unexpected breakthrough is upon you. Find yourself in His presence and get ready for His glory to be unleashed on every side and arena of your life.

Worship is the key that will invade and drive back the forces of darkness, making a way for the triumphant entrance of the power and glory of God into every area of your life and the advancing of His Kingdom. Worship will release the power of God with supernatural breakthroughs and manifestations of His greatness in our midst. As food is to the body, so is worship to your life.

If ever you want to overcome or reign in the midst of adversities, worship in your life is vital to see and live out God's purpose in victory. Just as a magnet attracts metal and commands it to come, so will worship attract the presence, glory, and favor of God on your life; the blessing will have no choice. It must come! It will overtake you! His glory will be released on those who love Him and carry His presence. The favor of God toward you is not based on your accomplishments, abilities, or inabilities.

Without hesitation, His favor will overtake the one who pursues Him. When you work, you expect to get paid. When you fail, you expect defeat. However, aligned with Christ, what the world expects will not define you. His presence will deliver an unexpected favor causing all blessings, favorable relationships (kings and queens), wealth, and prosperity to latch onto your very being. When you pursue His presence, you become a magnet for the favor of God to track you down. It's coming to you, Baby!

God understands the language of worship. In spite of our flaws, when His worship goes forth, His favor follows. If you are tired of being tired and find yourself overwhelmed by the pressures of life, then I invite you on this journey of worship that will change your life forever. You will find in these pages how worship has delivered, transformed, and brought healing to me. Through many adversities of setbacks, abuse, oppression, and sickness, God has abundantly delivered!

In a land of drought, famine, and monumental adversities, align yourself with the movement of God and position yourself to set your eyes on the Lord. Through the thresholds of worship, you will find yourself catapulted into a realm of living life victoriously. No matter the opposition, your circumstances and struggle will not determine or dictate your outcome. Let your perspective decree victory on every side because you have made the Lord your reward! In the position of pursuing Christ I declare and decree this to you in Jesus' name: *You*

PREFACE

shall advance in adversity. As your worship ascends, the glory of the Lord will invade your arena releasing to you all that He is. Every opposition will be eradicated as the Father skips over millions to see about you. God will show up in you, through you, and for you. This book will not only help you to survive. It will catapult you into His presence where the unexpected will overtake you. An anointing that destroys strongholds will suddenly come upon you. Your life will overflow with *multiplicity*, multiple breakthroughs. With Jesus in the boat, you can smile at the storm. Get ready to rise and ride the waves of adversities. You will conquer and overcome the odds. An unexpected advance is upon you!

Chapter One

WHERE IS MY DADDY?

AS A LITTLE girl about the age of three, I received the answer to a question that long awaited a response. "Where is my daddy?" And so my journey begins. My mother explained to me that before I was born my father became sick unto death. He was in the hospital, terminally ill with cancer, while she was expecting me in the delivery room.

On the day of my birth it was said that he crawled himself out of bed with the little strength left in him. He found his way over to the labor and delivery unit. He was on a mission to see his baby girl. Though he knew that he was on his last strength, he was determined to see his baby girl's face. After seeing me, and upon such a selfless act, he went home to be with the Lord.

What a dramatic story, and how it has haunted me many years to come. Filled with confusion, anger, and feelings of abandonment, I continued on a journey that awaited many adversities, trials, and triumphs. I was clueless to the extreme adversities that would soon confront me. Emotional trauma invaded my world and darkness flooded my thoughts. Something horrific had happened and fear had set out to cripple my ability to love, trust in another, and grow. Though unaware of my expected future, the adversities ahead, and the power to overcome them, God had a plan and He's made known my end from the beginning.

I developed a phobia toward all men and I cried relentlessly whenever left alone. I allowed myself to bond with no one, including the mother who nurtured me for many years to come. My mother did not understand my behavior and attributed it to some unusual temperament and that this child was just moody. My behavior, though obviously that of someone traumatized, was never taken seriously.

In an effort to protect myself, I separated myself from everyone. I had not yet learned that burying one's pain is never the answer for trauma or crisis. We must face and conquer our demons or they will come back again and again to haunt us. Upon my entrance into this world, I was hit with a fearsome blow. Day in and day out, life became painful, leaving me with a feeling of abandonment. I came into a world feeling completely rejected, but could not express it and neither could I understand it. I needed my daddy to walk with me, talk with me, carry me on his shoulder, and take my boo-boos away. I needed to hear his voice and gain his approval and cheers. The more I grew, the more the trouble came. Why did Daddy die? Couldn't he have waited? Did he really have to go?

So many of us are faced with abandonment, where our fathers are "missing in action." For some you were kicked to the curb. Not important enough. For others like me, Daddy was taken away via death or was incarcerated. Whatever the reason, there is a void that only a daddy can fill. No matter how hard you try or how well you behave, you find yourself faced with disappointment and emptiness. Longing, crying, praying . . . I want my daddy!

A man might even be present in the home and in the church (ooh!). But his love has vacated. His fatherly support is never to be seen, experienced, or embraced. He is "MIA" and you are left to search for him. With the feeling of rejection and abandonment you begin searching, only to hit roads of more turbulence and disappointments.

I've always stated that it's not about how strong or powerful the storm is, but how you react or handle the storm will determine its ability to destroy you. It's not the storm that kills you; it's your inability to conquer it or your inability to properly confront it that takes you out. Thank God that He didn't leave us ill-equipped. He has provided us with everything that pertains to life and godliness. And His desire is for you to walk in total healing and victory. As an heir to the throne, you have received power to tread over every opposing, anti-deliverance force that sets out to destroy or even distract the purposes and plans of the great and wonderful things God has prepared for you.

The Lord gives us a command to love Him and gives us the instructions to receiving Him: "Confess with your mouth and believe with your heart and you shall be saved." The latter portion states "believe." To believe is to be consistent in trusting that the outcome will deliver positive results in your favor. Trust will come out of a relationship that says, "I know your character, it speaks for itself;" therefore, in spite of appearances, the outcome will be for my good.

Through a relationship with the Father we now look ahead with new strength, new hope, and with new perspective in God's ability that He is love and He will perform, show up, and deliver His very best to us.

Pertinent to your destiny is to know Him and become one with Him. Communing with God is the highest purpose for which you were created. The Lord gently calls to you and you are challenged to do the same by reciprocating your love to Him through your life of worship.

When His presence becomes our passion and our passion is for His heart, we can boldly approach the throne of God with confidence that He loves, He hears, and He comes to our rescue. Your alignment gives you access and power to tread upon every adversity and dismantle every force of darkness that seemingly opposes you.

Your Steps Are Ordered

From the very end to your beginning, God has called your life into perfection, revealing all that He is. Before the beginning of time He was and is, and He is in control of it all. He is the author and finisher of all that is set before us. Along life's journey, all that you will encounter and every opposition that arises has already been written. Our heavenly Father has written the story and nothing takes Him by surprise. Through your questions of "why?" and "how come?" be assured that your life is in His hands and that Jesus cares, He sees, and He knows. His love covers you and He calls you on a journey that will transform you, reflecting all that He is.

Before the foundations of this world, God has hand chosen you to embark on a journey into the fullness of your destiny. Before you were born He knew you, and so your life unfolds from its end to its beginning. A victorious, wonderfully made, more than a conqueror, overcomer, abundantly blessed you.

> "Remember the former things, those of long ago; I am God, and there is no other; I am God, and there is none like me. I make known the end from the beginning, from ancient times, what is still to come."
>
> —Isaiah 46:9–10

> "Before I formed you in the womb I knew you,
> before you were born I set you apart."
> —Jeremiah 1:5

Before it all began, you were called and appointed to come forth. For such a time as this in your life—your story, your adversities, and your struggles—God has set you apart to be His light that shines in darkness. As you come forth, you will come out rightly equipped. With this challenge, I extend to you an invitation: Oh come, let us worship and bow down. Let us kneel before the Lord our Maker.

Your life will never be the same. Set yourself to run after God with all your heart. As you pursue Him, you will be empowered in His presence to face every opposition great and small. For in Him we live, move, and have our being.

Created to live as sons and daughters, created to reign as kings and priests. God has ordained you to live above the means. As you draw close to His heart, He will enter your arena and your life will never be the same. In Scripture, just as the ark of God rested on Obed-Edom's house, delivering an anointing of multiplicity and breakthroughs, so it will be for you.

You will discover that through worship, the forces of darkness will be driven back as the glory of the Almighty enters your atmosphere. A door will open that leads you to the advancing of God's Kingdom and the triumphant entry of His power into every area of your life. Worship will release a supernatural anointing of breakthrough, healing, and victory on every side that will cause you to overcome and reign as the king and priest He has called you to be. You will surely survive every storm, subdue them and triumphantly overcome them.

Destined To Overcome—Surviving The Womb

A baby's survival in the womb and its triumphant birth, when it announces, "Wha–a–a–ah! I am here! I'm alive!" models our walk as believers. After the stages of development and surviving the womb, the baby (who going forward I will call "Joy") must overcome the womb in order to transition through the birth canal and live.

Through the trimesters of pregnancy and through conception, development, and growth, Joy goes through a significant transformation. Each stage involves change and new abilities. Cells are continuously multiplied, and very soon after surviving the process, a beautiful, perfect, and wonderfully made baby pushes her way out of the womb (comfort zone), through the birth canal (place of extreme pressure) and is birthed (place of abundance).

As the due date approaches, the atmosphere and pressure in the womb becomes overwhelmingly uncomfortable. If Joy decides to stay in the womb, her life would soon end; she couldn't survive in the womb. Staying in her comfort zone would ultimately kill her. She must overcome the womb, pass through the birth canal, and be birthed in order to live and reign.

We are often distracted in our comfort zones. A comfort zone could be to us an atmosphere of things we are used to, whether it's good or bad. In the comfort zone we become afraid to welcome change or we are intimidated by the challenges set before us that will advance us from one level to another. We stay in the zone simply because we are accustomed to our surroundings. It's our place of safety, when in all truth it will become hazardous to our life and to our existence.

Most of us never make it past this stage; we choose to merely exist or survive, never growing or experiencing new levels. We accept life as is and never welcome life in abundance. There is a greater and better life available to you in Christ. We are not called just to live, but to live life abundantly.

> "The thief comes only to steal and kill and destroy; I have come that they might have life, and have it in the full."
> —John 10:10

The Fight of Your Life

In the birth canal Joy is fighting for her life. There is resistance on every side. However, she is on a mission: She must leave her comfort zone and transition to life out of the womb. She has survived the womb and now must overcome the canal that she may abundantly live. Though her pain and resistance of labor is on a colossal scale, she must advance and come forth. The pain radiates, her oxygen is decreased as seconds pass awaiting her arrival for that first breath. Through the excruciating difficulty, she squirms and presses her way to birthing. Simultaneously, mother's pain increases; she feels her intense pain and is urged to push. The pressure of Joy bearing down causes mother to give Joy a hand in the transition.

Together, Joy and mother go through the process of labor, and with that last push, Joy makes her entrance with shouts of praise to the Almighty, "Wha–ah, wha–ah! (Hallelujah)! God has delivered! I've overcome! O the celebration! Mother rejoices in the arrival of her newborn Joy. She's finally here. She has made it through!

The stages of pregnancy (place of expectation) and the trimesters, followed by labor and delivery, model the entry into the life we experience after the womb and our life after receiving Christ as Savior. After birth or salvation, we are faced with new opposition and experience growth upon growth. The questions are: Will you survive the pressures and adversities? Will you conquer the setbacks? Will you push through in spite of it all until victory is claimed and oppositions are conquered? Will you choose to worship your way through the pressure, receiving the breath of life that enables you to abundantly live?

While in the womb (place of comfort), and passing through the birth canal (place of extreme pressure), you are not alone. Just as the expectant mother nurtures the baby in the womb and feels the pain of contractions as delivery approaches. Mother helps Joy along the way and pushes her to delivery. In the same way, the Lord Jesus gives us all that we need to overcome the trials and adversities of life. He sees your tears, feels your pain and He wants you to overcome every obstacle; and through Him this becomes possible. As life flows from mom to baby through the umbilical cord, so life will flow to you through the cord of worshipping and having a relationship with the Father. Through the connection of worship (relationship), your life will be forever changed. Choose to make that connection and be empowered to overcome every opposition. The challenges in life will not overcome you when Jesus becomes your portion.

Just as Joy opens her mouth and lives, you are challenged to do the same. Push your way through the pressure, open up your mouth and live. Live, Baby! Live! Your journey begins!

God Has a Plan for You

You may survive the rain. You may survive the strong winds of life's storm. You survived the womb, but don't stop there. God is very aware of all that concerns you and His desire is for you to know Him in all His power and authority. You are more than a conqueror, an overcomer, called to show forth the Glory of God. Everything that happens to you just doesn't happen. His plans for you are for you to walk in divine destiny and that destiny is to know Him. Knowing Him gives you access to living life as an overcomer. Living life abundantly in total healing and victory is what He desires to give you.

> "For I know the plans I have for you," declares the Lord, "plans to prosper you and not to harm you, plans to give you hope and a future."
> —Jeremiah 29:11

The Lord loves us so much that He patiently waits for us to realize that without Him life is empty, and our need of Him is vital to our existence. Only in Christ we are made whole. Without Him we are incomplete and remain void with an emptiness inside that only Jesus can fill. It is in Him we receive strength and power to advance and overcome every obstacle. Only in Him will we experience satisfaction. His plan for us is victory on every side. His plan is for our future to experience His abundance. As we experience His mighty hand of deliverance and healing in our midst, we can now be a living testimony that God is able. He has delivered us and we can share with our neighbors He will also deliver them.

Shake off fear and discouragement and do not be dismayed. Clothe yourself with garments of worship and praise and watch every heaviness and high thing become leveled ground. For the battle is not yours; but it belongs to the Lord. You just have to trust Him, seek Him, and know Him. Jesus cares and He will come see about you—if you trust Him.

EXPECT THE UNEXPECTED

You Are Not a Victim but a Victor

You are not just a survivor—you are more than a conqueror. Getting through your adversities still leaves you with a victim mentality. You are not a victim, but you are a victor. Overcoming your adversity gives you victory because the adversity is defeated and you are on top of it. Don't just survive the storm and accept it as enough, but conquer your fear and eradicate the thing that attempts to destroy you. Through Christ you can receive victory over every struggle, limitation, and adversity.

With Jesus in the boat you can smile at the storm. This thing that you are struggling with, that attempts to destroy you: I declare that it won't work. No weapon formed against you, my sister, will prosper. No weapon formed against you, my brother, will prosper. "You will advance and you will win," declares the Lord Almighty.

Grab hold of the heart of God and what He desires for you. As you worship the Father and grasp His attention, you will be catapulted into His presence and liberated from yourself. Worship will bring you to a place of intimacy with the Lord and cause you to rise above every setback. With the Lord on your side you will conquer and defeat every extremity and impossibility of life that comes your way. Your adversities are no match for the Almighty God.

An Invitation to Know Him

"Now faith is the substance of things hoped for, the evidence of things not seen" (Hebrews 11:1). You have not seen it, but you hope for it because you know that it's on the way. With this confidence you can develop a lifestyle of worship to the Almighty God, knowing that all things work together for good and knowing that God is with you always and through Him you can do all things. God is sovereign and holy. He is the Creator of heaven and earth, the Alpha and Omega. The Beginning and the End. All wrapped up in one word, He is *love*.

Love protects, love is patient, and love gives its best. Jesus is absolutely crazy about you and He wants to give you the best. He wants you to come forth dressed for the occasion as the center of attention that says, "Wow, he or she is no doubt an heir to the throne, that's my child!" That individual just shines and reflects the glory of the King. The catch is, we must receive Him, walk with Him, and trust in Him. Receiving Jesus is the first step of knowing and loving Him. As the first and greatest commandment states: "Thou shalt love the Lord thy God with all thy heart" (KJV). Loving God can be accomplished only through Christ Jesus. Jesus said, "I am the way, the truth and the life."

Things of this world will never satisfy us; and we are not left without a resolution. The Word of God gives us the answer: "But seek ye first the Kingdom of God and His righteousness, and all these things will be added" (KJV). Victory and the power to overcome will rise within us as we set ourselves to trust in the Almighty God. We must first understand that the ability to trust God will only come through connection of knowing Him. This connection manifests itself as we relate to Him in worship.

Worship Defined

Previously defined, worship to God is attributing one's love—one's loyalty, service, compassion, affection, worth, confidence, and appreciation from his or her heart with unswerving faith, unswerving hope, and unswerving confidence that God is reliable and you can count on Him. Worship is for your advantage. Through trials and tribulations, distress and discouragement, broken marriages, physical abuse, rape, incest, bankruptcy, abandonment, sickness, and the list goes on. Worship to God coupled with faith states, Jesus is Lord of all and no matter what happens or the opposition, God is love! In Him and through Him you are more than a conqueror.

We have ultimate victory and that victory can be yours here and now. As you shift from taking your focus off your problem, reposition yourself to focus your eyes on Jesus. Let Jesus be your anchor and your deliverer. Let Him be your portion and your reward. Trust Him and never doubt, only believe! All things are possible to the one who believes. Watch and see what He will do.

THINK ON THESE THINGS

- Worship is first and foremost an encounter with the Almighty, Living, and Holy God.

- Worship is only as real as the involvement of the one participating.
- We should take advantage of every opportunity to praise God.
- Worship is submitting to God in obedience and bringing Him our very best, giving Him His worth.
- Worship, however is *not* just the lifting of hands, the opening of one's mouth, the shout of praise, or the clapping of one's hands. It is not just attending church services or reading one's Bible.
- Worship is more than religion, attending church services (ritualistic), or praying and fasting for one's benefit, whether personal or corporate.
- Worship is a lifestyle that gives to God His worth, knowing Him, trusting Him, and reflecting His character in all that He is and in all that you do.
- Worship is having genuine compassion. It is faith in action, reaching out to others in selfless love and servitude.

"Yet a time is coming and has now come when the true worshipers will worship the Father in spirit and truth, for they are the kind of worshipers the Father seeks. God is spirit, and his worshipers must worship in spirit and in truth."
—John 4:23–24

As we face and encounter the storms of life, let us press into His presence. Pursue Him with all your might, with all your heart, and with all your strength. Trust in Him always and see Him turn every impossibility into His ability. He is the Great I AM and His glory will come forth through you and for you.

Prayer

Father, in Jesus' name I pray for your daughter and son today. I specifically pray for those that faced physical, emotional, and sexual abuse at the hands of another. I also pray for those who have been emotionally hurt or discouraged by cruel and insensitive accusations. O God, I pray all of heaven would descend right now, this very moment, and surround them. Above all else, I pray that they will cast this pain and burden onto you. I pray that they will know that you love them and healing is theirs for the asking. Right now in the name of Jesus the forces of darkness and seeds of depression, hopelessness, and defeat that were released over their lives are rendered powerless. The Lord rebuke you, foul spirit of oppression! Release this daughter, release this son right now, in Jesus' name.

Now my friend, receive His love and worship Him. The healing begins. . .

Chapter Two

FACING LIFE'S GIANTS

LIFE IS FILLED with various trials and testings. For some, they are few. For others, "When it rains, it pours." As we encounter adversities or giants, they are destined to come down and we are destined to overthrow them. The Bible states that in our life we will have trials or giants. Thank God that giants do come down. They are not meant to destroy us, they will not defeat us, and the Lord will deliver us from them all. Not one of them will escape when we make the Lord our pursuit and passion.

After understanding my father's passing, I shortly encountered, at the age of three, an enormous giant. For a span of three years, I experienced a brutal, horrific encounter of sexual abuse at the hands of two relatives who were responsible to care for me. This giant had set out to destroy me and take me down, but God had a plan. The perpetrators had made me their personal playmate and did whatever was pleasing to them. The abuse caused within me confusion, anger, and deep hatred toward them and even my mother. I hated life, everything, and everyone. Within me I felt stripped of all dignity and self-esteem. Everything was my fault, including my father's illness and death.

Throughout the next three years, I was filled with fear and was tormented night and day. Physically, mentally, and emotionally I was hopelessly distraught. Yet, I couldn't run from it. Each time I encountered the giant, I froze. I couldn't move—there was no kicking, no screaming, and no emotion whatsoever. I often thought to myself, is something wrong with me? Though I was threatened not to say a word, couldn't I have stopped it? It was my entire fault! Everything was my fault! My mind ached, my body ached, and my soul ached. A serious cry for help was emanating from my very soul.

In many ways, I felt useless, hopeless, helpless, and completely defeated. I hated myself, hated life, and wished it were all a dream. If I could have buried myself, I would have. Wanting my daddy and knowing that he was forever gone caused me an inner pain and tremendous anger that I couldn't run away from. I felt completely deserted and alone. The pain and fear was constant and nothing I tried eased it. My cries for help with tears and unusual behavior toward men along with my introverted personality were to no avail and no one heard or recognized them as a serious cry for help. Under normal circumstances a child would play as not having a care in this world, but for me, there was no laughter, no joy, and no giggles. I earnestly yearned for a place where I couldn't feel. The hurt and pain were too overbearing.

Before long, I began to inflict pain upon myself as an attempt to somehow relieve the inner turmoil that was tearing me apart. My tears continued night after night as did the abuse. I felt trapped and thoughts of dying flooded my head. I was in desperate need of a supernatural intervention. I was on my way down to self-destruct. Little did I know that from the very beginning, the Lord had a plan and certainly all of heaven heard every cry. My cries were not in vain.

No matter what has happened or is happening, one thing is sure—Jesus loves you and He cares. Your pain is real and yes it hurts beyond words can express. He knows and sees every tear, He feels every pain, and He understands every struggle and trauma that confronts you. I know that the burden is heavy. I know that the pain is real because I have lived it. The Jesus in me tells me that He will bring you out and His love will restore to you all that the Enemy has besieged. The earth is the Lord's and the fullness thereof. There is nothing too big, no mountain too high, no pain too deep that He cannot heal, and no brokenness that He cannot mend. There is no setback or struggle that can keep you away from His love. Draw near Him, for He is knocking at your heart's door.

No Matter What Has Happened, God Cares

In life we encounter many difficult calamities. Many times they are at no fault of our own. We often experience adversities in great proportions and find ourselves asking the question "Where is God? And does He love me?" Well! Fret not, dear Daughter and Son. The Lord is very near and He loves you; He awaits your acceptance of His invitation to draw near Him. Make Him your love connection and you will soon realize that His love is unfailing. There is nothing that will take you away from the awesome love He has for you.

You may not understand why you go through what you go through, but be not dismayed. You are not alone and God will not allow anything to destroy you, for there is divine purpose on your life. You may have faced abuse or have suffered loss or maybe even rejected by those closest to you. Things may look real dark for you, but be encouraged and know that the battle belongs to the Lord and He won't let you down. There is nothing in life that can stop you, separate you, or strip you of your dignity when you are positioned to see Christ as He sees you.

> Who shall separate us from the love of Christ? Shall trouble or hardship or persecution or famine or nakedness or danger or sword?. . . . No, in all these things we are more than conquerors through Him who loved us. For I am persuaded that neither death nor life, neither angel nor demons, neither the present nor the future,

nor any powers, neither height nor depth, nor anything else in all creation, will be able to separate us from the love of God that is in Christ Jesus our Lord.

—Romans 8:35, 37–39

These promises are available to each of us when the Lord becomes our pursuit, our passion, and our everything. Let's take a look at the story of David and Goliath.

Imagine David approaching Goliath. David is a misfit, an unsuspecting match to take on a giant named Goliath. He's small built, unequipped with the proper armor. Yet he stands before Goliath willing to take him on and bring him down. What were his thoughts? What will I do? Could I defeat this monster of a man? Can little me defeat this giant of an enemy?

When we face the giants of our lives, we may say to ourselves, this thing is too big for me. I don't think that it will work out. I don't know how to get out of this mess. We are "in a recession." I'm losing my house, can't make my car payments. I lost my job. I have a major illness. I just can't make it through. My situation is a losing battle and besides I just can't go on. It's too much for me to handle.

All of that spells no hope and breathes negativity. This kind of attitude will keep you in a position that expects failure. With such a perspective, you've just set yourself up for a losing battle. I encourage you to shake off and uproot seeds of defeat and set yourself in a new direction that declares, "You are more than a conqueror," and nothing will separate you from God's love. You will conquer the impossible and what's expected will not define your outcome. Through Christ, you will attain the unexpected and soar to heights unknown to man or woman. In the process of the pain, never let the Devil see you sweat! Come hail, wind, or flood, you will not be defeated. But you shall live and advance!

Learn to Trust God

Having confidence in someone comes out of a trust you have developed through the relationship of knowing him or her. David had a relationship with God; he knew his God and was very confident in God's ability to deliver him. When He saw his giant, he didn't react with doubt or hopelessness. But, rather, he stood up in faith and confidence that God would deliver and fight his battle. He saw victory and saw himself as the victor and not the victim. David declared:

> "The LORD who delivered me from the paw of the lion and the paw of the bear will deliver me from the hand of this Philistine (1Samuel 17:37).... This day the LORD will hand you over to me, and I'll strike you down and cut off your head."
> —17:46

Though suppressed on every side with adversities, you will not die, but live. The devil is a liar. God says you will win. You will survive the storm and you will live the life of an overcomer. Equip yourself with knowing truth and as the old hymn says, believe this:

> My hope is built on nothing less than Jesus' blood and righteousness.
> I dare not trust the sweetest frame but wholly lean on Jesus' name.
> On Christ the solid Rock I stand, all other ground is sinking sand.

Make the Lord Jesus your hope. On Him, you will stand. David looked at his giant. Yes he saw his aggression, his fearsome looks and overpowering size. Goliath was equipped for the battle: sword, shield, and all. David said to himself, I may not have a physical armor as this giant, but I have the armor of God and surely God will deliver.

Your battle or adversity will not be won by a physical sword, weapon, or armor. It will be won only with the armor of God. The armor of God will be your shield, sword, and victory!

Put On the Whole Armor of God

If it's raining hard and you don't have a shelter, then it is certain that you'll get soaked. If the storm is raging and your ship is not properly equipped; then for sure you'd be shipwrecked.

When we are not properly equipped in our endeavors, pursuits, and challenges, we limit our chances of surviving, much more, overcoming. This is why we must equip ourselves with what the Bible describes as the whole armor of God. In a nutshell, "the armor of God" describes the true meaning of worship.

We must put on the whole armor of God that we may be effective in battle. We must first align ourselves through a personal relationship with the Lord. Second we equip ourselves. Third, with God all things are possible. The power to conquer and overcome every adversity is set before us.

> Finally, be strong in the Lord and in His mighty power. Put on the full armor of God so that you can take your stand against the devil's schemes. For our struggle is not against flesh and blood, but against the rulers, against the authorities, against the powers of this dark world and against the spiritual forces of evil in the heavenly realms. Therefore put on the full armor of God, so that when the day of evil comes, you may be able to stand your ground, and after you have done everything to stand. Stand firm then, with the belt of truth buckled around your waist, with the breastplate of righteousness in place, and with your feet fitted with the readiness that comes from the gospel of peace. In addition to all this, take up the shield of faith, with which you can extinguish all the flaming arrows of the evil one. Take the helmet of salvation and the sword of the Spirit, which is the word of God. And pray in the Spirit on all occasions with all kinds of prayers and requests. With this in mind, be alert and always keep on praying for all the saints.
> —Ephesians 6:10–18

Throughout my life as a believer, these passages have been my rear guard. As with David, God's Word has helped me overcome adversity upon adversity. It truly models what a lifestyle of worship represents. Hold on to it, practice it, and live it! You will not be disappointed.

God's Armor for Us

- The *belt*—used for truth. The Devil fights with lies and sometimes they appear very real. We need God's truth to defeat the lies of the Devil. Know what God says concerning you.
- The *breastplate*—used for righteousness. The Devil mainly attacks our heart, the place of our emotions, self-esteem, and confidence. The righteousness of God protects our hearts and gives us God's approval. We are His righteousness. His righteousness defends us. Know that His love covers you and approves you.
- The *footgear*—used to spread the gospel with readiness. The Devil tries to immobilize us from telling others of God's goodness. He tries to shut our mouth from proclaiming what God has done and how He can deliver others. We should always be ready to share with another how God has delivered us.

- The *shield*—used for faith. The attacks of the Enemy appear very real in our eyes. Persecutions, setbacks, temptations, sickness are all felt and seen as they are encountered. The shield of faith will protect us from the Enemy's flaming arrows. With God's perspective, we can see beyond our adversities and know that ultimate victory is ours. The situation may look like this, but God says that. He says victory.
- The *helmet*—used for salvation. The Devil gives suggestions to make us doubt the ability of God and all He has given us. The helmet will protect our mind from doubting the saving work of God. This is where most battles are won. Never accept the lies of the Enemy that says that you cannot win, but hold on to hope. Protect your mind by reminding yourself of His promises.
- The *sword*—represents the Word of God. The sword is the only weapon of offense. There comes a time when we must take action and offense against the Enemy. The Kingdom of God must take offense against the attacks of the Enemy and silence him once and for all.
- *Prayer*—used to strengthen your relationship with the Lord. Through prayer a close relationship is developed and your confidence in the Almighty is strengthened. With this

confidence, you know that nothing will stand against you.

When David faced his giants, his victory or ability to overcome was based on his perspective. His knowledge of God and his belief in the Almighty God to fight his battles were unswerving. Your belief or perspective will result on your relationship with the one you trust. His view on who God is and what God can do delivered David to victory every time. His pursuit of God and trust in the Almighty kept him certain that no weapon formed against him would prosper, and against all odds, he knew that he would win. He knew that he would advance. There was no demon in hell, giant, person, or obstacle that would stand in his way of victory.

It's all on how you see it. In the face of opposition, your perspective or response should not be, this thing is so big that it will absolutely destroy me. But your response should be, this thing is so big that my sling can't miss it! My God will wipe it out, take it down, and blow it to smithereens. He's my defender and He has crushed the head of every enemy and foe. Adversity, I decree to you that you are coming down!

You Can Depend on God

Let God do it and let us learn from the example of David. David pursued God with his entire being. He understood the true meaning of worship and therefore, he was able to face every giant and defeat every foe. He lived the life of an overcomer and conqueror simply through his lifestyle of worship. His relationship with the Father reflected his worship and confidence of the Father's ability to deliver. He trusted in His faithfulness and power to always show up.

It is absolutely essential that as we walk our journey to His Kingdom that we cultivate a personal walk with God. Through this walk we will learn how to trust Him, love Him, and serve Him. As we walk with the Father, we will advance, overthrow, and conquer every enemy and darkness that sets out to destroy us. Our enemies will be placed under our feet where they belong. We will go forth as we lift Jesus above every circumstance. We must dethrone and bring down every obstacle that keeps us in a place of defeat. Let His presence infuse you and give you strength to advance. His glory will defend your story and give you victory.

> "Arise, shine, for thy light has come and the glory of the Lord is risen upon thee."
> —Isaiah 60:1 KJV

When His glory becomes your story, every giant will come down. Your adversity is no match for God's authority. Expect victory and never let an impossible situation intimidate you. Your attitude will determine your outcome, not your circumstance. Embrace the Lord and lean on His promises. Watch Him do the rest!

Look at your battle and declare to it that God will do it. David declared in the presence of all the onlookers what God will do. In doing this, he automatically set the atmosphere for God to enter, show up, and show out. He said to the onlookers:

> "All those gathered here will know that it is not by sword or spear that the Lord saves, for the battle is the LORD's, and He will give all of you into our hands."
> —1 Samuel 17:47

Make the Lord your portion as David did and claim every promise. His confidence in God came out of a relationship with God. Just as God did it before, David knew, He would do it again. Build your hope on the Lord Jesus Christ. He won't fail you, and He will not let you down.

Prayer

Father, in Jesus' name I pray for your daughter and son today. I specifically pray for those that are overwhelmed by the many giants of life. I also pray for their minds that they will be released right now from every thought of defeat that says to them that they cannot make it. O God, I pray all of heaven would descend right now, this very moment, and surround them with power from on high. Above all else, I pray that they will know that there is nothing too hard for you. I pray deliverance from every giant that has set out to steal, kill, and destroy. Right now in the name of Jesus the forces of darkness and seeds of depression, hopelessness, and defeat that were released over their lives are rendered powerless. The Lord rebuke you, foul spirit of besiegement, intimidation, and hopelessness; release this daughter, release this son right now in Jesus' name.

Now my friend, receive His love and worship Him.

Chapter Three

STRENGTHENED IN HIS PRESENCE

I STARTED GOING TO Sunday school, and on my seventh birthday I was introduced to Jesus. I was excited about all the great things He has done and how vast His love for us expands. I was frequently picked up via the church van and I eagerly awaited the arrival of each session. These sessions gave me a sense of hope and escape from my pain.

However small your service in the kingdom of God may appear, never despise it. You are sowing a tremendous seed that will produce a harvest. Never despise small beginnings. You may be the greeter at the door. Your smile and "Good Morning, God bless you" accomplishes more than you can imagine. Everything you do, do as unto the Lord and do it cheerfully. Serve the Lord with gladness and know that your serving is not in vain. Keep on sowing those seeds. The harvest will come if you faint not.

Having Jesus in my life gave me a new outlook on life. Attending Sunday school was most refreshing. Singing and praising God lifted me to a place I did not think existed. Unaware of the transformation that was taking place, the love of Jesus was changing me. Compassion for others in my heart began to grow and this was strange since that I hadn't cared for anyone or anything. My heart began to open and something marvelous was unfolding.

As I have taught my own children how to worship, I have prayed and hoped that they, too, have experienced the transforming power of God's love and the joyous effect of giving God our worship. My daughter, who is six years old, has expressed to me after Sunday's worship, "Oh, Mommy, today was my bestest day ever." I would ask her what about it makes it so special and she would respond, "I sang to Jesus, I clapped my hands, I lifted my hands, and I closed my eyes. I feel really good, Mommy." Those words were so pleasing to my ear. How beautiful it is that even a child can experience and understand the power of worship.

Worship releases us from ourselves as His presence fills our heart. Worship will treasure God's presence. It will humble the heart, extend His love, it will give, and the same time expects God to respond. Hebrews 11:6 states it like this; "He who comes to God must believe that He is, and that He is a rewarder of those who diligently seek Him."

Foremost, worship is God's gift to us. It is for our blessing and benefit. It is not our gift to Him.

Sunday school also taught me how to pray and I learned quickly. I prayed earnestly, consistently, and fervently. For the first time I knew that my tears and my cries were being heard. I knew that Jesus loves me just as I am and His love wasn't based on my past or shortcomings. I am so glad that I came to Jesus as I was. Just as you are, you can, too. God doesn't seek the saved (when I get it together) or those who think, I'm good the way I am. He comes to save the lost and He receives you *as is*, with great benefits and a warranty guaranteed! He backs you up 100% and transforms you to face and conquer any road.

My knowledge of Him grew and I desired more and more of Him. I did not want religion or tradition; I wanted God in a very real way and was determined to have Him. I am persuaded that when our hearts are stirred to love God, an entrance for the Almighty is made in our lives for the King of Kings to take center stage enthroned in our very hearts and in our surroundings. With God on the throne of our lives, every mountain is made low, every valley exalted, and every high thing that exalts itself above Him is brought down. God desires to enter your arena of life's struggles, setbacks, and adversities. He desires to manifest Himself in all power, glory, and supernatural ability in and through our lives.

Now, what's in store for me? I believe God, I trust God, I serve God, and the pain is still there. It's still very real and I can't run from it. I thought

God would take it away! Well, Friend, news flash. God wants to bring you through the Valley. He will not just take it away. We must learn to trust Him in spite of what it feels like, looks like, or what it be like. As you find yourself in His presence, you are transformed and receive new strength to overcome and conquer all that seems impossible.

Today, right now in the midst of worship, He is invading adversities and setbacks. As worship ascends, God transcends His glory in power upon us and amongst us. He reveals Himself in greatness and sovereignty, transforming lives, families, and nations. He is eternally glorious and sovereign. Nothing is impossible with Him. Above all power, above all nations, and above all pain.

In all His greatness, He still awaits our welcome to work on our behalf. He is a gentleman and will not show up uninvited. You must consciously decide that you want Him in your life to be Lord and Savior. And when you do, get ready!

Hunger for His Presence

By this time I had developed an appetite for the Word of God through Scripture memory verses. Parents, your children are not too young for personal devotions. Instruct them, pray with them, and let them pray too. It will build their faith and personal walk with God. Teach them to worship God with you, and show them by example how to worship. Allow your children to partake and attend revival services when they are young. You will be amazed how the hunger of God will stir within them.

My children actively participate in worship and enjoy being in the presence of the Lord. My heart rejoices when my son, who is ten years old, approaches the altar with hands upraised and tears running down his eyes, all for the touch of Jesus. My daughter has run to me when I stubbed my toe, laying her hands on me and praying, "God, heal Mommy." If ever something bothers her, she asks "Mommy, will you pray with me?" I have often peeked into my son's room at bedtime without him sensing my presence and there he has been, sitting up with his Bible, just hungry to understand the Scriptures. In the morning, he approaches me with all his questions.

Scriptures and songs like "Yes, Jesus loves me" are favorites for our worship. Another favorite is "God is." The Lord is our strength, He removes all pain, misery, and strife. He keeps His word and stands on it.Oh, what power is delivered through these songs, and how much they have spoken to me time and again.

Scripture memory verses are also a part: "I can do all things through Christ who gives me strength".... "When I am weak, Jesus is strong"... "Greater is He that is in me than he that is in the world".... "And we know that all things work together for good to them that love the Lord and are called according to His purpose." Wow! I could go on and on!

Our children will take our cues when we lead them by example. The same void and emptiness within us is within them and they, too, need to experience God's love and grace. Pull them into worship and your Bible study times. Encourage them to pray, read their Bible, and develop a lifestyle of worship. After all, we do want the best for them, right? Then teach them.

What we say and the life we live are truly powerful. I often teach children that knowledge is power. Delight yourself in God's Word, lap it up, and soak it up. And always be mindful of the words that are released from your mouth. Your words carry power, so use them wisely. Never tear down another, but always build up with positive words of encouragement. Speak life to every dead situation and see it resuscitate and come back to life.

I desired more of God and longed to be in His presence every chance permitted. Sunday school was the only place I found peace and refuge from the torment I faced. I soon realized that I could pray and talk to Jesus any time, any day, and for any reason. I felt alive whenever in His presence and began to live the testimony of the Scripture that says, "The joy of the Lord is my strength." Prayer soon became my daily pursuit. I prayed like a child receiving the best Christmas gift ever, one that never wears out. Well! I prayed and I prayed. I found renewed strength and began to prove the Scriptures to be true at the tender age of seven.

Though my pain was very real, the comfort I found in Jesus was more real. The sexual abuse of the men that handled me had come to a stop but the pain, fear, and torment lurked in every corner. My tears slowly subsided and little by little I would intermingle with others. Allowing others into my world was a new challenge, but with God all things are possible. His love in me grew and it opened many doors of great friendships and support.

I have learned that prayer truly changes things. Set yourself to commune with God. Tell Him your struggles and see Him release His glory, enabling you to rise above the pressure and overcome the fear. Believing is good, but we must start acting on His promises. Begin by declaring His goodness over your life.

In Matthew 6:9–13 Jesus taught us how to pray.

Pray in this Manner

- "Our Father in Heaven . . ." Approach Jesus in your prayer and worship, knowing that He is your Father; the Creator who made all is all.
- "Hallowed be your name." Begin to worship Him. Acknowledge His sovereignty, greatness, holiness and power, who He is and what He has done.
- "Forgive us. . ." Ask for forgiveness, forgive others, and receive new strength to face each day.

- "Your kingdom come. Your will be done on earth as it is in heaven." Invite Him into your arena. Ask Him for all that He is to invade your earthly dwelling, needs, and desires.

Run After Christ, Not Traditon or Religion

Without Christ we are inclined to follow the way of the world, traditions, and religions. We claim that our allegiance is to God, but yet we continue living in darkness, just existing with no life insight. We choose to stay in the comforts of what we have read or learned from our forefathers, never engaging in a personal encounter with God, knowing Him, or trusting Him. For too long we have settled for tradition rather than a heart-to-heart engagement with the Father. Instead of personally pursuing Christ, we rely on our pastors, church services, and testimonies of our forefathers to bring us or expose us to a glimpse of His glory. It is time to break the tradition of traditions and run after God with all our hearts.

To enter worship with lip service is tradition. We must discard the old wineskin in order for fresh wine and fresh oil to be poured in. When our hearts are far from God, tradition is prevalent. Our allegiance or worship to Him is subjected to our needs, and giving Him worship as long as we are good or we have a pressing need.

> He replied, "Isaiah was right when he prophesied about you hypocrites; as it is written: 'These

people honor me with their lips, but their hearts are far from me. They worship me in vain: their teachings are but rules taught by men.'"
—Mark 7:6-7

Worship and prayer open a doorway to the power of God's presence. Not religion, not tradition, and not the coattails of our forefathers. Only in His presence there is life; no sickness, disease, affliction, or barrier could stand in His presence. His presence confounds dark powers, principalities, and spiritual wickedness. His presence destroys and overthrows every destructive operation of sin and darkness. His presence dethrones everything we've placed above Him and keeps us in bondage. God will work mightily when we align with His presence. When He is enthroned in our lives, expect and anticipate His move. God is able and He is waiting for our acceptance of His invitation to enter in. He will do more than we can imagine.

Now unto Him who is able to do exceedingly abundantly above all that we ask or think, according to the power that works in us, to Him be glory in the church by Christ Jesus to all generations, forever and ever. Amen.
—Ephesians 3:20-21

God desires a relationship with you. He doesn't want to be your magic button that you press every time you are in need. He desires to be everything, and waits with arms opened wide for us to run to

Him. Sometimes our present circumstances cause us to run away from God. Instead of running away, let us run towards Him and see His glory come down.

> Delight yourself in the Lord and He will give you the desires of your heart.
> —Psalm 37:4

> "He who has my commandments and keeps them, it is he who loves me. And he who loves me will be loved by my Father, and I will love him and manifest myself to him."
> —John 14:21

Jesus promised this out of His love for us: "Never will I forsake you" (Hebrews 13:5). And "Surely I am with you always" (Matthew 28:20). He gives an invitation to worship God in a way that brings about a personal intimacy and relationship that states, "I am my beloved's and He is mine. His banner over me is love."

Jesus' invitation says, "Come and I will give you rest. Receive me and learn of me." The weight of life's pressure will be lifted as we receive Him.

Loving God is the heart of worship. Will you love Him simply because He is God? In Mark 12:28–34, Jesus explains that the greatest commandment of all is to love God with all our heart, soul, mind, and strength. There is a level of praise and adoration that pursues God just because of who He is. And it is available to those who dare press in deeper to His heart. Loving Him with everything you are and every moment of the day. Not just because of what He has done, but simply because He is God. Will you abandon yourself to a radical, reckless, passionate love for Him? When you find a love in your life, it is only natural to want to be in the beloved's presence. Find yourself in a love relationship with the Lord. You will find that your greatest happiness is being in His presence.

In the beginning God created because He loved. He so loved the world that He gave us His only Son. Spoken out of Himself, the Word became flesh and lived with us. Jesus gave His life so that we through Him might have everlasting life. All of this because of love. Love keeps you even when you are being torn apart. Love comes running to your rescue even when it is mistreated. Love covers; it protects and it gives you its best. The greatest of all is love and God is love. We are commanded to love the Lord with all our heart. Why? Because God is love. He loves us, and when we love Him we receive the benefits of who He is. In short, God loves us so much and desires us to receive and love Him that we may live. The only way is through Christ and to know Him is to love Him. Through your knowledge of who He is, you are compelled to worship, honor, reverence, and love Him simply because of who He is. Your worship to God is propelled through your love for Him.

Worship extols the Almighty. Worship is pursuing His very presence, running after all that He is and communing with Him in a heart-to-heart fellowship. Most importantly, it is a means of entering into a role of partnership with God's greatness. When you worship and when you pray, do it with a sense of expectation, expecting the supernatural and anticipating the intervention of God to manifest His glory with signs and wonders following. My friend, draw near to God. As you draw near, He draws close and the forces of darkness are driven away. Become filled with His presence and allow Him to invade and drive back every spirit of limitation, intimidation, barrenness, lack, and accusations that say you cannot overcome.

You will overcome and the love of the Father will get you there. I often tell the congregation, what you are passionate about you will pursue. When you love, you are compelled to give your best, your all, and your very heart. To love the Lord with all your heart, mind, and strength is to know Him. Get in His presence, read the Word of God and develop your knowledge of the Father. See His love stir your heart into a love relationship you never thought possible. His love for you will burn within you, causing a chain reaction that ignites you to return the love. Larnelle Harris' song "I Miss My Time with You" speaks words of a powerful love relationship between the Lord and you. This song has drawn me each time I find myself drifting away from His presence. The words imply that Jesus longs to fellowship with you but you are too busy with the cares of life, ministry, and personal struggles. With our minds so preoccupied, God says how? How can you love Me and serve Me when deep inside you are void and empty?

What's in your hand may appear insignificant and small. You may think that you don't have much to offer. But God calls us to come to Him just as we are. Our service and giftings may appear small. Again, never despise small beginnings. God wants you right where you are and just as you are. He longs for more than just your good morning or goodnight prayers. He longs for more than the sacrifice you give Him on Sunday morning and midweek Bible study. He longs for more than just a part of you; He desires you wholly. He longs to commune with you—and get this—not for His benefit, but for yours. He loves you because He loves you. How profound, God loves because He is love. To know Him is to love Him and to love Him is to know Him. To live you must love Him and when you love Him you live. Simply amazing! His love is beyond my understanding. To love Him as He loves me is what I desire. Make the Lord your every pursuit. Love Him with all your heart and position yourself for overflow as His love infuses your very being.

Prayer

Father, in Jesus' name I pray for Your daughter and son today. I specifically pray for those that are struggling in their life of prayer and devotion to You. I also pray for their hearts that they will be renewed right now, that their minds will be cleansed, and that the sins and yokes of bondage that hold them will release them right now. You will no longer be entangled with them. O, God, I pray all of heaven would descend right now, this very moment, and surround them with power from on high. Above all else, I pray that they will pursue You with all their heart and love You always. Right now in the name of Jesus the forces of darkness, distractions, and seeds of false humility and pride that take residence over their lives are rendered powerless. The Lord rebuke you, foul spirit of religion; release this daughter, release this son right now in Jesus' name.

Now my friend, receive His love and worship Him.

Chapter Four

KEEP ON MOVING AND DON'T STOP

WHEN I WAS about eight years old, a crusade was being held in town. I attended one midday service with the Sunday school kids and during the call for salvation I felt compelled to find myself at the front line. Although I had already committed to Jesus, I wanted to make a public stand confessing Jesus as my Lord. I made the Lord my pursuit and found myself in His presence every chance I got. I believed with all my heart that Jesus saves. This however, did not cause my pain to instantly evaporate. There were moments of setbacks and fearful flashbacks that still haunted me. So I resolved to pray and worship and always found renewed strength in His presence.

God Is Waiting for a Yes

God uses the vessel that's available to Him. He sees the heart that longs after Him. Never is greatness due to one's own ability. "It's not by might, nor by power, but my Spirit," saith the Lord. There are men and women of God who have done many great and mighty things in the Kingdom with signs and wonders following. But never is it by one's own strength. With this in mind, run after God with your whole heart and let His greatness manifest through you. Your answer should be, "Yes, Lord, nevertheless, not my will but Your will be done in me."

Greatness came, and still comes, to men and women of God along with the passion and desire for more and more of Jesus. God will work through those who believe and trust Him. We must never think we've "made it" and proclaim personal power or ability when it's a result of God-given success and doings.

Whenever we obey God, success comes. Let us make certain that we know that it is all by the strengthening of the Spirit of God and not our own. When you make God your everything, He becomes your everything.

In my times of distress and adversity, my only release is in Jesus. No matter how hard I try in myself to get past my loneliness, pain, or struggle, I never seem to quite overcome them if I try in my own strength. I often find myself battling the same demon again and again.

When we choose to handle our adversities alone, we eventually become discouraged and depressed to the point of giving up and losing our minds. If we are not careful to give our cares to the Lord, they will consume our being and lead us down a road of self-destruction.

When I find myself in distress where my back is against the wall, I break out in worship and set my mind on Christ. My worship to God releases me from myself. As I press into worship with tears flowing, I cry out, "Lord, I need You." There is nothing in life that will completely satisfy or fill the void that only He can fill. I would call to God to fill me with His presence. "Draw me close to You, Lord. Hold me and wrap me in Your arms. Please keep me close to Your heart and never let me go."

My heart then begins to sing of His goodness. "Lord, You are my joy. There is no one in all the earth that satisfies like You. There is nothing I desire besides You. For You are great and none can compare to You." As I press into His presence, my heart cries out for more of Him. "You are everything to me. Take me deeper in You. In Your presence is where I want to be. Just to be close to You is what my heart desires." Redirecting my attention to the Lord in times of discouragement brings healing to my inner man. I find renewed strength for the day, my faith is strengthened, and I gain new perspective that God is on the throne and He will deliver.

I remember one year I broke my arm in multiple locations and was rushed to the emergency. When I arrived, they did not know what to do with me. I was so trained to praise God in adversity that automatically I started to bless God, laughing and praising through the pain. One of my sisters accompanied me, and to her surprise she couldn't believe my response. The entire staff on call gathered around me in amazement. I was not crying or screaming. I was praising God. Praise will cause you to refocus. The giant before you comes tumbling down when worship is released.

As David did, I learned the secret to pursuing the heart of God. Jesus is the blood that keeps my heart pumping. He is the reason why I live and breathe. He is the answer for my every crisis, the lifter of my head. He is the peace that passes all understanding. My joy, my friend, and the Lover of my soul. He is my everything.

Through worship I have learned to trust in Jesus. I have learned that worrying over something I cannot change is a waste of my energy. Why not rejoice in the Lord and let Him handle it? I have proven Him true over and over that He will fight my battle when I take up my position of worship.

With God all things are possible and nothing shall be impossible. Don't allow discouragement and even religion silence you or deter you from pursuing Christ and doing the work He has called you to. When in battle or facing opposition, stand firm and don't sway, stick to the plan of His Word. Be confident that as you pursue Him: He advances you and will always deliver. Remind yourself of His faithfulness and love Him always.

> "I love you, O LORD, my strength. The Lord is my rock, my fortress and my deliverer; My God is my rock, in whom I take refuge. He is my shield and the horn of my salvation, my stronghold. I call to the LORD, who is worthy of praise, and I am saved from my enemies."
> —Psalm 18:1-3

> "You, O LORD, keep my lamp burning, my God turns my darkness into light."
> —Psalm 18:28

The Lord will keep you consistent and He will turn your problems to possibilities. Everything that is big or seems impossible to work out, He enables me to overcome it. Psalm 18:33 promises, "He makes my feet like the feet of a deer; he enables me to stand on the heights." He enables me to stand and maneuver on every rough terrain, giving me "all-wheel drive" to overcome every stormy path and rough terrain.

Press On and Press In

We are not called to give up. We are called to obey and pursue Him whatever the cost. You may have hit a hard place in your life or ministry, but don't you give up. Don't offer excuses to yourself, but *pray*! Excuses will rob you every time of your inheritance. We must not continue to blame others for our mishaps or excuse our inabilities as the fault of others.

Use your authority in Christ, calling those things that are not as though they were. Never allow defeat to take residence in your life; instead claim *all* of God's promises and expect the manifestation. He will keep every spoken Word, for His promises are "yea" and "amen." He will not sleep or slumber on His watch. He works exceedingly, abundantly above all you can imagine. Don't bow to setbacks. Pursue the Lord with all your heart. Pursue Him with all your strength. Pursue Him with all your soul. Run after Him. He is the fuel in your engine. He is your life.

David encouraged himself time and again by setting His eyes upon the Lord and seeking after God:

> O God, you are my God, Earnestly I seek you; my soul thirsts for you, my body longs for you, in a dry and weary land where there is no water. I have seen you in the sanctuary and beheld your power and your glory. Because your love is better than life, my lips will glorify you.
>
> I will praise you as long as I live, and in your name I will lift up my hands. My soul will be satisfied as with the richest of foods; with singing lips my mouth will praise you.
> —Psalm 63

Though pressed on every side, David's desire was to make the Lord his pursuit. His first resort was Christ. Notice I did not say "last resort." David thirsted for God because nothing else would satisfy. He states his soul would be satisfied as with food when He blesses the Lord with songs of praise. More than anything else, he clung unto God's love because it brought to him something that this world could never deliver.

In spite of the pressures and storms, David was determined to press on and press into the presence of God. Like gold or anointing oil, a person needs to go through the refining process to come forth polished, spotless, pure, strong, and resilient. A tree being cut down goes through extreme pressure. It is bruised and bent, and it goes through a rigorous process to become lumber that becomes part of a home's foundation that will soon be transformed into a spectacular dream home or strong structure. Extreme pressure—extreme transformation. Don't fight the pressure, conquer it and subdue it! Do not bend, bow, or break down against the pressures of life. Instead, resist and refute every lie and flaming arrow that is thrown at you. The finished product will be a sight to behold! Pursue His presence, advance in adversity, survive the storm and live as an overcomer.

Strongholds Are Difficult but Not Impossible

Personal addictions, struggles, and strongholds will always have the tendency to rob us or delay us from living in the fullness that we are destined to. For this reason, we are strongly encouraged to cast down such imaginations and all things that place themselves above the knowledge and authority of God. We may think to ourselves that this addiction is impossible to break or get past, but we must stand firm on the Word of God and daily renew our minds that we may be able to look at every struggle with the determination that nothing is too difficult when we make the Lord our source and strength. It's all about choice: Do you want to release this thing that doesn't please God? Or do you want to hold on to it because it pleases you?

It is true that some things are absolutely difficult to let go, much less give them all up. Reason being, the spirit is willing but the flesh is weak. As long as the flesh (human desires) dictate your next move, you will always find yourself living after those desires. When we allow His presence to infuse us, the power of the Holy Spirit takes the lead and in spite of the struggle we are empowered to overcome and move to the next level. Our fleshly nature or human desire should always be subject to the spirit man. Only in worship, sincere and broken worship, is this made possible.

When I find myself struggling with an attitude or action that does not please God, I must make a conscious decision to pursue Christ and not allow the "thorn in the flesh" as Paul described to control me. If we don't take the bull by the horn, that bull will certainly stare us mad onto a road of destruction.

In times of my personal thorns, worship to the Father has kept me focused and tamed. Yes sometimes I go off course, but I'm immediately drawn back by His love to stay on track.

As long as you are a living soul, you will face trials, and I'm speaking of trials that deal with the personal you that no one else sees, the thing or struggle that has you in bondage behind locked doors and the stronghold that you just can't seem to knock down. Some realities exist that we may never shake off, but God gives us the strength and grace to overcome them and dethrone them when we put our faith and trust in Him. Therefore our life of worship is key to overcoming the fleshly struggles and strongholds that keeps us imprisoned and bound. At most, those thorns or stumbling blocks God allows, that we may be reminded that in ourselves we are weak and need the strengthening of the Holy Ghost to advance.

> "See, I lay in Zion a stone that causes men to stumble and a rock that makes them fall, and the one who trusts in him will never be put to shame."
> —Romans 9:33

I understand that it's difficult, but you will get through this as you make the Lord your portion. He will make a way of escape for you to handle it. Choose to set your affection on the Lord and I assure you that every stronghold will be made low. Note this: I said "made low." Strongholds, thoughts, and every high thing that exalts itself above God is our responsibility to take captive and subdue. Paul explains it clearly:

> I know that nothing good lives in me, that is, in my sinful nature. For I have the desire to do what is good, but I cannot carry it out. For what I do is not the good I want to do, no, the evil I do not want to do—this I keep on doing. . . . So I find this law at work: when I want to do good, evil is right there with me. For in my inner being I delight in God's law. . . .
> —Romans 7:18-22

> Therefore, I urge you, brothers in view of God's mercy, to offer your bodies as living sacrifices, holy and pleasing to God—this is your spiritual act of worship. Do not conform any longer to the pattern of this world, but be transformed by the renewing of your mind.
> —Romans 12:1–2

> We demolish arguments and every pretension that sets itself up against the knowledge of God, and we take captive every thought to make it obedient to Christ.
> —2 Corinthians 10:5

I could go on and on with verses that illustrate our struggles and the many excuses that we make for ourselves why it's OK or God understands. The fact still remains that sin is sin and God does not condone it. It is only through belief in Christ, giving our lives as a living sacrifice, and entering in His courts with worship that we are justified and freed from the entanglements of sin. Overcoming is very active. Yes, the battle is the Lord's, but obedience is our duty and it is not at all passive. We must act/react in order to advance. Whatever the addiction may be—sex, alcohol, drugs, gluttony, shopping, pornography, manipulation, or anger—we must turn our eyes to the Lord and be steadfast in our pursuit of Him or these strongholds will continue to grip us and delay our destiny.

> . . . till I entered the sanctuary of God; then I understood their final destiny.
> —Psalm 73:17

Until you enter in, you will never fulfill purpose and walk in destiny. Distractions will always present themselves, causing you to remain stagnant. In Christ we are justified as He *re–members* us (puts back together) and we, in turn, *re-present* our lives through the glory of the Cross that so shines within us. In His presence, then and only then, we are empowered to let our light so shine before others that they may see our good works and glorify our Father in heaven (Matthew 5:16). I encourage you to stop making excuses and lift up your head that the King of Glory may come in.

It's funny how sometimes we pray and ask God, "O, please, help me not to sin or do this thing," when God is waiting for us to make the decision that we will not continue in spite of the strong desire to satisfy the flesh. When we make the decision to do the right thing, we will receive empowerment to resist every opposition and temptation. We must make the decision that we will not allow the pressures of life, thorns of the flesh, or sin keep us from the Father. Shall tribulation or distress or peril or sword separate us? Nothing shall be able to separate us from the love of Christ! Set yourself to tear down every stronghold and stay determined that no element will control you, no weakness or struggle of the flesh shall have authority over you.

> Lift up your heads, O ye gates; be lifted up, you ancient doors, that the King of glory may come in. Who is this King of glory? The LORD strong and mighty, the LORD mighty in battle.
> —Psalm 24:7–8

You shall subdue nations, problems, struggles, and impossibilities; and they shall submit to the Spirit of Christ that lives in you. The Lord longs to come in that you may be the more than a conqueror and overcomer, He has ordained you to be. Won't you let Him?

Prayer

Father, in Jesus' name I pray for Your daughter and son today. I specifically pray for those that are pressing into You in spite of adversities. I also pray for renewed strength and a supernatural push of Your anointing that will catapult them to their next level in You. O God, I pray all of heaven would descend right now, this very moment, and surround them with power from on high. Above all else, I pray that they will run after You with all their heart and love You with a reckless abandonment of themselves. Right now in the name of Jesus the forces of darkness, demonic strongholds, barriers, and limitations that have crippled their ability to move forward are rendered powerless. The Lord rebuke you, foul spirit of distraction; release this daughter, release this son right now in Jesus' name.

Now my friend, receive His love and worship Him.

Chapter Five

WORSHIP CHANGES THE ATMOSPHERE

IN THE EARLY '70s when I was growing up, crusades and revivals were quite common. There were men and women of God sharing the gospel just about on every corner. A revival was approaching and I wanted very much to partake of God's move. I just had to get there. Having an unbelieving parent made it difficult to get there on my own, and I was too young to commute and was often deterred. Though deterred, I would have a praise celebration on my own. I was determined to worship God in everything and in every way.

One day I got dressed and went out on the front porch waiting for my pick-up (church bus). It was a beautiful day and the sun was shining bright. The birds were singing and my mind drifted to how great God is. My mother and stepfather saw me waiting and became frustrated at my eagerness to always be in church. Infuriated at my persistence, I was called back into the house. It was difficult for them to understand why I was so eager to go to church. They would often remark, "It won't kill you if you miss a service." Sometimes I would be scolded, ridiculed, and sent to my room. Oh, but God. . . it didn't last long and that didn't stop me. Hallelujah, anyhow.

My desire was to run after God like my life depended on it. And it did. I made God my top priority and refused to let Him go. Like David, a God chaser and man after God's own heart, I had to seek Him, and I was determined to run after God with everything within me. David's greatest desire was to know God and do His will. He walked in daily fellowship with God and loved God with a burning passion and reckless abandonment.

We must let go of everything in our lives that could challenge God for first place or hinder our pursuit of Him. Follow after Him and you will not be disappointed. He will come see about you, for after all, you are His beloved.

Worship is the salt of all power. God's power and purposes in our lives and the restoration of His rule on earth happen through the power of worship.

> Then the eleven disciples went away into Galilee, to the mountain where Jesus had told them to go. When they saw Him, they worshiped Him; but some doubted. And Jesus came to them and said, "All authority in heaven and earth has been given to me. Therefore go and make disciples of all

nations, baptizing them in the name of the Father and of the Son and of the Holy Spirit, teaching then to obey everything I have commanded you. And surely I am with you always, to the very end of the age."

—Matthew 28:16–20

There is tremendous power in worship that causes the Lord to dwell among us in power. As we abide in worship, He will not only dwell in our midst, but will infuse His life and His Kingdom to rule among us, transforming lives and administrating His Kingdom on earth. The atmosphere around us will adapt and change in submission to the presence of the Lord. His presence will cause all fear and doubt to acknowledge His Lordship. Rendering the hearts of people and frustrations powerless as they bow to His authority. "All authority in heaven and in earth has been given me." Authority to overcome and command things that are not as though they are is released to us. Turning the hearts of man and circumstances to work in our favor.

Though my mother could not understand my urgency to be in His presence. Her misunderstanding could not stop, deter, or interrupt my longing or the tangible communication between the Lord and me. Not even the bitterness, anger, pain, nor myself could keep me back from experiencing His presence. Where the Spirit of the Lord is there is significant life, restoration, and tremendous opportunities for breakthrough. Our position is to set our eyes upon the Lord and as He is enthroned over our atmosphere, everything else must submit. I thank God that I learned this secret at the time I did. Knowing the truth that Jesus is Lord and constantly pressing into His presence has delivered to me on every level victory, healing, and the power to overcome in spite of my present dilemma. I have learned to declare daily that my name is "Victory" because Jesus is my Lord. There is nothing that has the power to overcome you when Jesus is Lord. The atmosphere must change when Jesus is enthroned in our lives.

The creation waits in eager expectation for the sons of God to be revealed. For the creation was subjected to frustration, not by its own choice, but by the will of the one who subjected it, in hope that the creation itself will be liberated from its bondage to decay and brought into the glorious freedom of the children of God. (Romans 8:19-21)

There is a sound of worship that will summon the power of God, causing the whole of creation to reflect His glory. In expectation, the atmosphere waits for the sons and daughters of God to take up their position of worship.

ENCOURAGEMENT FOR WORSHIP LEADERS

Praise and worship as a body is very vital to the growth and life of the church. We gather together to worship and have fellowship one with another. Without true worship, we would just experience the latter. Lives would remain stagnant and church growth would dwindle. Before long, the congregation would become lifeless and congregants would come out as a formality. If true worship were not released, the church would eventually die with just the building and the faithful few that regularly attend services, living just to exist. The quickest avenue to experience victory, healing, and restoration is through worship.

Let us retrace our steps toward worship once again. Worship is giving God our very best. It gives to God His worth. In total surrender to Him, we release all our needs, struggles, resources, and abilities. In the process, we expect Him to move on our behalf.

Leaders, you cannot stand as a worshiper who gives God second best. In some cases, He receives an "I don't feel like it" praise, a "We can just blow through" praise or sometimes a "Just doing what is expected of me" praise. This kind of worship is completely selfish and does not give to God the glory due Him. It is arrogant, geared to oneself and positively does not touch the heart of God. Our worship to God should be broken and selfless, giving to God the glory due Him. Do you really believe that God would accept such an offering? Think about it. Would you accept a gift from a loved one that's dirty, torn, used, and has the stench or appearance of trash? I'm certain you would throw it out, maybe even right in front of the giver.

Now, why would you give your gift, the gift of yourself, to God as if it were garbage? When you stand to worship, your worship should transcend your mood, your feelings, and your worries. Regardless of how you feel or how the congregation responds, worship should break past yourself and take you to a level of honest, broken worship, to a place where nothing else matters. Your worship should go forth with shouts of acclamation that God is good. In spite of your disposition, exalt His name and tell of His goodness. Open your mouth and your heart. Lift up your head and let the King of glory come in.

As a worship leader, if you want to see a radical transformation take place in your worship services, approach the throne abandoning all else and give to God your very best. Choose to give God sincere praise and the atmosphere will change. God inhabits, moves, and dwells in the atmosphere of worship. Where there is true worship, God is in the midst. On another note, the congregation is looking and waiting on you. They will eventually respond and join in when your worship is consistent and sincere. Before you know it, praise will permeate the entire room. Some of you might be laid out on the floor, so watch out. Praise is contagious!

Let us not allow ourselves or those around us to dictate the worth we give to God. If God is worthy, then let us worship Him in spite of the appearances of our surroundings or the pressures that confront us. Give to Him the praise and honor that is due Him. Give to Him your absolute best!

WORSHIP CHANGES THE ATMOSPHERE

Worship Will Release You

Have you ever been lied about or persecuted for something you didn't do? What about something you did do? Well! The power of God's grace through our worship will dissolve and condemn every tongue that rises against you in judgment.

The experience of Paul and Silas in the Philippi jail teaches us that worship will break the chains of darkness and bondage including accusations. Paul and Silas were about the Lord's business and were thrown in jail. They were beaten, bound, and stripped of every dignity they had. Despite this dismal situation, they resolved to praise and worship God. It's pretty easy to pursue the Lord or shout praises when everything is going well. Praise becomes easy when there's no opposition. In a dark situation or midnight crisis, the Lord says to you, "Fear not," but open your mouth and sing forth My praises. Make His praise glorious and watch what He will do.

> About midnight, Paul and Silas were praying and singing hymns to God, and the other prisoners were listening to them. Suddenly there was such a violent earthquake that the foundations of the prison were shaken. At once all the prison doors flew open, and everybody's chains came loose.
> —Acts 16: 25–26

You may have gotten yourself into trouble by breaking the law. You may have been falsely accused of something that doesn't reflect you. Or you may have done something that you are guilty of. Regardless of the facts, His grace is sufficient to release you and bring you to victory. If any man be in Christ, he is made new. The past and the present facts do not determine your future. Only in Christ is this possible. Man will always move by what is seen. God looks at the future and that future is for you to overcome and have success.

Don't hold on to the guilt of what you have done, but rather release it to Jesus and forgive yourself. Holding on to the chains of condemnation will keep you bound. The Bible states that no matter what you've done, if you surrender it all to God, there is no condemnation to you. Forget about it and run after God. Press towards Christ even in the midst of your struggle and He will transform you. He will turn your situation around and do the unexpected. What has set out to destroy you will not destroy you, but will work for your good when you release it.

When you fall, don't stop there, get up with the determination that you are more than a conqueror and you can do this. I declare that you will conquer this thing. Position yourself to worship God and you will be released. While in the process, your praise will also free somebody else. True worship will change the atmosphere.

Where worship is released, God's presence comes to dwell, and where God's presence dwells, there will be power. In His presence, the works of darkness are

WORSHIP CHANGES THE ATMOSPHERE

frustrated. The Enemy's plans are dismantled and the operations of hell are counterattacked.

Imagine coming out to a worship service where sincere praise is being offered. A divine and supernatural anointing is released where bodies are healed. Cancer, diabetes, high blood pressure, broken bones, and tumors are all instantaneously eradicated, gone, nuked. Hallelujah, glory to God! This is the kind of atmosphere that will be released when we release ourselves to His presence. Better yet, imagine walking in such a place of communion that your very shadow releases an anointing for divine healing and breakthroughs. Oh, how I look forward to this kind of revival! And it is upon us as we draw near His throne. I declare that I am in there and you, too, can be a part of this divine move of God, if you choose His presence. Where worship is released, His presence dwells, and in His presence there is power!

As the glory of the Lord showed up in Obed-Edom's house because of the ark of the covenant and blessed him and his entire household; so will the glory of the Lord overtake you when you worship.

David understood the dynamics of worship and began to worship God with all his might:

"David, wearing a linen ephod, danced before the LORD with all his might, while he and the entire house of Israel brought up the ark of the LORD with shouts and the sound of trumpets" (2 Samuel 6:14–15). All around Him households were being blessed and those who opposed or despised the worship of God were cursed and unfruitful. "As the ark of the Lord was entering the City of David, Michal daughter of Saul watched from a window. And when she saw King David leaping and dancing before the Lord, she despised him in her heart" (2 Samuel 6:16).

Michal's' attitude or position to worship God was blinded by bitterness and it caused her to lose her inheritance. We often become bitter or angry when things don't work out according to our plans, but be careful to never curse yourself by despising the person of God, His Kingdom, or His servants. David had set his mind to worship God with all His might because it was the Lord who had chosen him, anointed him, and delivered him. God could have chosen another, but He chose me and I will worship even if it makes me appear as a fool. "It was before the Lord, who chose me rather than your father or anyone from his house when he appointed me ruler over the Lord's people Israel—I will celebrate before the Lord. I will become even more undignified than this, and I will be humiliated in my own eyes" (2 Samuel 6:21–22).

God understands the language of worship, and releases His glory upon those who are after His heart. In those who have learned to worship and those in whom God has restored fellowship, the power of His greatness is relinquished to liberate the captives. In the midst of that fellowship God will reveal Himself, His awesome majesty, and His mighty power.

When faced with a threat, persecution, or midnight crisis: choose to rise up in worship. Instead of being preoccupied with the problem, worship God and declare to the problem that God is above all and He will deliver. Worship will push you to victory and will ignite the atmosphere as if some explosion occurred. Every distraction will be rerouted and transformed to declare God's glory.

PRAYER

Father, in Jesus' name I pray for Your daughter and son today. I specifically pray for those that know and love You and are dealing with various adversities and discouragements. I pray that their strength will be renewed right now and that You send divine intervention to work in their favor. O God, I pray all of heaven would descend right now, this very moment and surround them with power and favor from on high. Above all else, I pray that they will continually praise You and press into You, in spite of opposition. I pray restoration to every area that is experiencing limitation and bondage. Right now in the name of Jesus the forces of darkness and seeds of lack, famine, and barrenness are rendered powerless over your lives. The Lord rebuke, you foul spirit of besiegement and bitterness; release this daughter, release this son right now in Jesus' name.

Now my friend, receive His love and worship Him.

Chapter Six

HOLY GHOST POWER TO ADVANCE

THE CRUSADES IN my hometown were still ongoing and I prayed earnestly that I would get there. Well! Through Holy Ghost intervention, the church sent a special invitation and requested for me to come out and participate in the program. I could sing my little heart out and found great joy in every opportunity to share His love. When I opened my mouth the atmosphere would change and the Spirit of God would move. Well! I made it to one of the Holy Ghost Revivals and oh, dear, was I in for the surprise of my life. I was ten years old and was aware of the gift and power of the Holy Ghost. I have witnessed individuals overcoming seemingly impossible situations through the power of His Spirit. I purposed to myself that I would receive Him. I must have Him! I wanted the Holy Ghost like a kid wanting candy. It tastes so good that you just can't get enough.

When we line up through worship as the disciples did on the day of Pentecost; and seek the Lord in one accord. Their lives were empowered by the Holy Ghost and a tremendous shift took place in their ministry. Ministry for them went forth with greater power and manifestations of God's glory and power. Likewise, your life will be empowered and a major shift will occur. Your life will go forth with greater power and manifestations of God's glory (Acts 2:1–4.)

Infilling of the Holy Ghost

I desired this experience and power and prayed for the Holy Ghost passionately. Well! I got there and I remember it like it just happened. Second row left side of the sanctuary. The sanctuary was beautifully adorned and worship permeated the atmosphere. I worshiped, tears running down my eyes. I was ready like yesterday and felt a fire burning within me to open my mouth.

Tears and more tears covered my face and there was such a burning that surrounded me. With a burst, my mouth opened up and words and languages unknown to me filled the house. Intermittingly English and tongues flowed. There were words of affirmation and declaration for both the church and me. I was familiar with this operation of the Spirit but never did I expect such an outpouring on little me.

At the conclusion of the service I was unaware of all the gifts that flowed in that session. The glory of God and unction of the Holy Ghost moved upon me in various areas: tongues and interpretation of tongues, word of knowledge, and revelation as the Holy Spirit gave the utterance. Wow! I remained in a place of total spiritual bliss for about three days and no one, no one, could get in between. It was a sweet holy communion.

I thank God for those experiences because it shows me that God will use anyone who is ready, willing, and obedient. In spite of your failures, God will work through you, if you let Him. His blessings are available to those who want it. Are you willing to also pay the cost? Or are you only interested in reaping the harvest? There's plenty of loot to harvest. There's also our part to labor. Most of us get too comfortable in life. So comfortable that we choose to merely exist and accept things the way they are. We say to ourselves, "Hey. . .it is what it is." But not so! Man shall not live by bread alone, but by every word that proceeds out of the mouth of God. What you want, Jesus got it. What you need, Jesus got it. All He asks is that you seek Him.

How Bad Do You Want It?

God will use anyone that makes Him his or her pursuit. The same Holy Ghost that filled me then continues to fill me and imparts to me strength and truth. The same Holy Ghost is available to you today, right now. If you are seeking the Holy Ghost or desire a recharge, He can be yours right now. Just ask in faith and open your mouth. Matter of fact, why not take a worship break and allow His presence to infuse you with power from on high. Release to God sincere worship and your desire for the Holy Ghost and get ready, get ready.

During several revivals, I've had the opportunity to minister on the topic of the Holy Ghost. Each time, God showed up and believers were filled. Many times, they were so eager for the Holy Ghost that I barely walked by and there they went. Services that involve "tarrying" I stay clear from. In my own experience, too much of self (emotion) is involved. My preference is to teach, making certain that the level of understanding is clear, deliver what "thus says the Lord" and expect the supernatural manifestation of His power to take residence.

I often share with others that we are the same and God's favor follows the one that delights in Him. Each of us has the opportunity for greatness. Each of us has the ability to overcome our adversities. Each of us has the doorway of God's favor and supernatural access available to us. But we must pursue Him. Ask and it shall be given. Seek and you will find. Knock and it will be opened.

After you ask, don't stop there, though the answer is given you must still pursue until you have possession. Seek and you will find. Research and understand the thing that you have asked for. You cannot use what you don't know you have. Even after you receive the thing you ask for, you must educate yourself on its ability in order to make full use of it. Now knocking or pressing in brings it into your possession. When the door is opened then access is granted. The answer is simple and the question is elementary. Do you want it or not? If you do, then get in line and move with His cloud. The cloud of His glory. Stop relying on self-skills, education, and abilities and let God empower you. Ask in faith, believing it's yours; seek and get the understanding; knock and take possession. Let the Holy Ghost empower you.

From then on, my pastor had his eyes on me. Most important, the hand of the Lord was upon me. My pastor acknowledged the hand of God was heavily on my life and through counsel and the laying on of hands I began a fresh journey of ministry, winning souls for Christ and showing the love of God in everything I set out to do.

Whatever I did from then on was never the same. I desired to only move as the Lord led me and never to do anything in self-strength. Each time I ministered, the glory of God filled the house, souls were saved, people were healed, strongholds were destroyed, and yokes and bondages were broken.

Signs and Wonders Following

Through the ages of ten and twenty-one, I ministered at many revivals. Numerous healings and deliverances took place. One occasion I remember so clearly; it was at a three-night revival international missionary trip. A woman who had a heart condition was instantly healed when I called her out. I saw the whole thing flash before my eyes. The anointing of God was heavy in that place. People were being healed and delivered all around, but this one was pressed heavily on my heart. It was as if I saw God perform open heart surgery right before my very eyes. She returned the following night and testified of how God had healed her. During her preparatory visit, her surgery was cancelled, as there was nothing wrong with her heart. I was in awe of God's power and the accuracy of people's individual crises. A man also testified that he was a drug user and addict, and instantly, while I was ministering, the power of God came over him and he knew that he would never touch the stuff again. Today, that same man is serving God and pastors a church. Hallelujah!

Having the opportunity to minister recently at various revivals, God has been faithful even in the midst of my flaws. There was a time I felt that I had to be absolutely perfect and often found myself in a place of condemnation. I would resist myself from preaching or sharing His love based on guilt and personal inadequacies. The Scripture states "resist the devil and he will flee." Instead I was resisting the move of God. Who was I kidding? Joke was on me I suppose. My heart's desire is always "Lord use me," and I learned that my "goodness" or "good behavior" will never cause God to work for me. Like so many of us, we limit the move of God in our lives simply because we resist Him. His love is limitless and has no boundaries; He only asks that we trust Him, know Him, and seek Him. His glory and manifested presence is never based on our ability or inability. It is the anointing that destroys yokes. It is the power of the Holy Ghost!

The glory of the Lord has been released on many evangelistic revivals. Before ministering the Word, my prayer is Lord move amongst your children today and give them just what they need. The power of His Spirit has never failed me, bodies healed, lives restored and souls saved every time. Not because of who I am, but because of Whose I am. In the midst of personal pain, struggles, and set backs, I have recently stood on pulpits where God delivered miraculously on every occasion. Mind blowing miracles and divine manifestations of His presence in the hearts of those who harbor unforgiveness, bitterness, and rage. The more God showers on me His love and correction, the greater I long to pursue Him.

We should never get weary in doing right. Even in our wrong, we should never get comfortable in embracing it as right. Learn to trust God step by step, one day at a time. Don't allow discouragement, people, mistakes, or even yourself keep you from running after His heart. Always set your eyes on the Lord and He will do the rest. Your expectancy should always declare God You are able, and in spite of how it looks or where I am, things are turning around for my good. He is more than able, Sovereign and Mighty! He will always work the impossible to possible, the intangible to tangible, the inability to

His ability. Though it is apparent that your situation is going in the wrong direction or your steps forward seem two steps backward. Be encouraged and know that God is working for your good and He's turning it around. I tell you the truth, He's turning it around!

Holy Ghost Explosion

I remembered visiting a Christian youth convention where no one knew me. I wanted to be refreshed and had a strong desire to bask in His presence. I received the getaway as a gift to be ministered to since I was coping with a recent broken engagement (relationship). Heartbreak is quite a roller coaster. It sends you for a loop! My fiancé at the time got cold feet and walked away. I thought to myself, it's going to be all right and this, too, shall pass.

Well! When I got there, it wasn't long before the anointing on my life was recognized. The guest speaker, a heavily built, tall man of European descent, called me out and ushered me up to the front during an altar call for those seeking the Holy Ghost. He grabbed my hand, moving me quickly in leaps and bounds with my hands slapping heads and laying (so it seemed) tongues of fire on each head I touched. Young people all around were receiving the baptism of the Holy Ghost. It was a Holy Ghost explosion!

All around me young adults and teenagers were being filled with the Holy Ghost. Some were dropping like flies as I walked by them and some went off into a holy laughter. Just laughing . . . it was quite hilarious and a sight to behold. The lives of those young people as well as my own were forever changed. Having experienced the power of God in such an intense way, we were filled with zeal, ready to take on the world.

Upon the conclusion of that convention I went home. The anointing still lay heavily upon me. I was so tickled by the power of God that when I arrived and the door was opened, I embraced my mother in the Gospel and we both went to the ground as some lightning had knocked us off our feet. Some friends were over and when I approached them and asked, "Do you want to experience God?" they looked at me baffled as if to say, "What is wrong with this child?"

I replied, "Watch this." I raised my hand and waved it and there they went, drop, drop, drop, to the ground. Fumbling and barely standing, they attempted to recollect themselves as if drunk with wine.

The rest was history; we had a refreshing time in worship and laughter. Ministry modeling these experiences has continued throughout my life. I have witnessed the power of God time and again with many healings and supernatural manifestations. These experiences, or rather a way of life, are also available to you today. The supernatural move and manifestation of the Holy Ghost will abide and reside with us when we devote to a life of much prayer and consecration. Not just in words or deeds, but in sincere, heartfelt worship to the King.

His peace that passes all understanding is available to comfort every sorrow. Most important, the Joy of the Lord will sustain you in the midst of confusion and uncertainty. When nothing makes sense and you are unable to see clearly, remind yourself that His strength is made perfect when you are weak. There is nothing you encounter that God isn't aware of. Nothing takes Him by surprise. As the Good Shepherd, He goes before the sheep, making certain that the path taken will not harm you but help you. Every weapon the Enemy sends to destroy you, God will turn it around. The seeming distraction now becomes a tool for God's glory and a gift for your benefit. Remember it's all on your perspective.

My trip to the youth revival was just a means to get away and reposition my thoughts. Instead God was up to something unexpected. I certainly did not expect to experience His love and presence to this degree. The Lord will always give you what you need, when you need it and how you need it. He knows His children and will pour into them all that He is. Something about the Holy Ghost, I can't explain it. He gets sweeter and sweeter with every new day. Our relationship is like "fire shut up in my bones"! What a time of refreshing and how much it was needed. He may not come when you want Him, but He is always on time.

Prayer

Father, in Jesus' name I pray for Your daughter and son today. I specifically pray for those that are seeking Your face for strength to press on. I also pray for a double portion of Your anointing to fall upon them right now giving them boldness and the supernatural unction of the Holy Ghost to conquer every adversity and overcome it. O God, I pray all of heaven would descend right now, this very moment and surround them with power from on high. Above all else, I pray that they will seek after You with all their heart. Endow them with Holy Ghost power and anointing. I pray for a fresh infilling of the Holy Ghost with the evidence of speaking in tongues. Right now in the name of Jesus let Your fire fall and remove every thing that is not like You. The Lord rebuke you, foul spirit of intimidation; release this daughter, release this son right now in Jesus' name.

Now my friend, receive His love and worship Him.

Chapter Seven

THE SETUP FOR THE COMEBACK

WELL! COLLEGE LIFE is great, having fun, enjoying the life. I'm dating and experiencing the life of an independent adult. During this time I started to have sleep disturbances and unusual demonic attacks of hearing voices and my childhood abuse replaying as though it was happening all over again. Oh dear God, help me! was my cry. Along with this new attack came other setbacks, one of which was experiencing a flood of my entire neighborhood due to heavy rain and a broken dam.

I just got my first apartment and I worked hard to furnish it. It was finally done—walls cream colored, black sofa and love seat. Delicately designed glass dinette, small office area, well put away. My bedroom reflected a white silhouette that gracefully flowed with the wind. Just my touch, it was beautiful, and it was my home.

It was about 12:05 in the morning and I was fast asleep, getting a much-needed rest to replenish me to report to work. Bam bam. There were knocks on my door waking me out of the deep sleep.

I stepped out of bed feeling giddy and unbalanced. I was puzzled because I stepped into water, which ran through my apartment. I went to the bathroom and there was water. The toilet was not running over and the pipes wee shut tight. I went to the kitchen and there was water. The sink was clean and the pipe was turned off. What is happening? I thought to myself. I ran to the living room to see through the window.

Bam bam bam—the knocks continued. "Ma'am, please. We must get you out now!" It was some firemen. I ran to the door and they yelled out, "Move away from the door!" The door swung open and with a great big gush water forced itself in, knocking everything over in its way. (This reminds me of the power of God when His Spirit moves. The power and glory of God will knock every obstacle out of the way. No opposition, force, or barrier could stand before Him.)

I was grabbed and taken to higher ground. (How significant in itself.) God was up to something. Well! I lost everything! All my hard work, all gone in seconds. Talk about a hard blow. People were crying everywhere. No fatalities though . . . to God be the glory.

THE SETUP FOR THE COMEBACK

Many times we are faced with circumstances where just when it seems that we have a foot on our lives and we are moving ahead, we find ourselves back in the same pit struggling with the same thing. Never producing, never advancing and taking ground. I believe that when we shout in the face of adversity and worship, God will show up. He will pass over millions of others just to come anoint you and see about you. When the storm comes you will stand firm. When the wind blows, you will not sway but you will stand and move forward against all odds.

Setbacks or adversities are truly opportunities for God's work to take center stage. In the face of discouragement, opening our mouths unabashedly to give God thanks and bless His name isn't easy. However, when we are determined to give God glory in the midst of those times, we will see the glory of the Lord begin to break forth. Every obstacle will be subdued, storms of life will calm, and the peace of God will reign. His peace that passes all understanding will keep your heart and your life.

> "Sing, O barren, you who have not borne! Break forth into singing, and cry aloud, you who have not labored with child! For more are the children of the desolate than the children of the married woman," says the LORD.
> "Enlarge the place of your tent, and let them stretch out the curtains of your dwellings; do not spare; lengthen your cords, and strengthen your stakes.

> "For you shall expand to the right and to the left, and your descendants will inherit the nations, and make the desolate cities inhabited.
>
> "Do not fear, for you will not be ashamed; nor be disgraced, for you will not be put to shame; for you will forget the shame of your youth, and will not remember the reproach of your widowhood anymore. For your Maker is your husband, the LORD of hosts is His Name; and your Redeemer is the Holy One of Israel; He is called the God of the whole earth."
>
> —Isaiah 54:1–5 NKJV

At some point in our lives, we all experience barrenness, where everything is at a standstill and no growth seems to occur. As you shout in worship you shall expand to the left and to the right. In Israel's barren situation, the Lord says, "Sing and shout and you will be expanded."

He tells Israel that her baby is on the way. Not just one baby but two, for you shall expand to the left and to the right. To sweeten the blessing, God says that fruitfulness will also come from those offspring. The blessing or breakthrough will not stop at you. It will pass on to you and your children's children.

My friend, do not fear, for you will not be put to shame. This setback will soon be behind you and you will go forth in victory. Your setbacks are God's opportunities to work out the impossible, making it possible. When He works, He does the *extra-ordinary* for us. His glory isn't just revealed through you, He reveals it for you.

What a powerful passage and message is unfolded here. I had the opportunity to preach this message on a few occasions and did God show up! He showed up and then some. Breakthroughs and restoration were instantaneous. I love it when God does a "suddenly." In the name of Jesus, I decree that as you open your mouth in adoration to the Lord an anointing of the "suddenly" will come upon you to release, restore, and resuscitate all that is barren in your life. I decree and declare to you today that every barrenness or lack must cease and desist. In a land of famine, I decree that you will prosper. In an economy that is in a downward trend, I decree that you will be successful. In failure and setbacks you will not be ashamed but you will advance. Enlarge the place of your dwelling and get ready for the expansion God is releasing. Prophesy to your barren land, your bank accounts, your careers, and the gas pumps, and decree that you shall expand and overflow with the glory of God. All the earth will see and know that Jesus is Lord.

Well! The Lord set me up real good. The Devil meant it for evil, but God turned it around for my good. I received such favor that I didn't know what to do with myself. After the transition period of sleeping in a shelter and finding refuge in homes of individuals I once ministered to, I received double for everything that was lost and destroyed by the waters.

I was placed in a new apartment—get this—with free rent for six months and it was three times the of the other one. Instead of a one bedroom I received a three bedroom. I received brand new furniture that I personally picked out. A new wardrobe, my first car, and food pantry items were also thrown in. New! New! New! Wow! God is never late! He shows up just when you need Him and gives you the overflow, full and running over. As we trust in the Lord and delight ourselves in Him, He will give us the desires of our hearts.

The Battle Belongs to the Lord

Take a look at Jehoshaphat (2 Chronicles 20) facing a vast army that has threatened to take him out. Though fearful and troubled, he resolved to inquire of the Lord. Upon his obedience and repositioned attitude of praise and worship, he and all his singers began to sing praises to the King of kings. The word of the Lord came to him saying:

> "Thus says the Lord to you: 'Do not be afraid nor dismayed because of this great multitude, for the battle is not yours, but God's. Tomorrow go down against them. . . . You will not have to fight in this battle. Position yourselves, stand still and see the salvation of the Lord, who is with you, O Judah and Jerusalem! Do not fear or be dismayed; tomorrow go out against them, for the Lord is with you.'" And Jehoshaphat bowed his head with his face to the ground, and all Judah and the inhabitants of Jerusalem bowed before the Lord, worshipping the Lord. Then some Levites from the Kohathites and Korahites stood

up and praised the LORD, the God of Israel, with very loud voice.

—2 Chronicles 20:15-19

The presence of the Lord will always drive out the forces of darkness. In His presence there is fullness of joy, life, prosperity, victory, and power. Worship confuses the Enemy and will dismantle the works of darkness. Where the Spirit of the Lord is, darkness flees; therefore, any and everything that is anti- who Jesus is must come down and remain down. For at the name of Jesus every knee shall bow. That's right—every struggle, adversity, and opposition that sets about to snuff out the Jesus in you must bow and confess that Jesus is Lord. During their worship with voices raised loud and high, the Bible says that every enemy was defeated.

> As they began to sing and praise, the LORD set ambushes against the men of Ammon and Moab and Mount Seir who were invading Judah, and they were defeated.... When the men of Judah came to the place that overlooks the desert and looked toward the vast army, they saw only dead bodies lying on the ground; no one had escaped. So Jehoshaphat and his men went to carry off their plunder, and they found among them a great amount of equipment and clothing and also articles of value—more than they could take away. There was so much plunder that it took three days to collect it.
>
> —2 Chronicles 20: 22, 24–25

EXPECT THE UNEXPECTED

The Power of Worship

The enemies of Jehoshaphat took themselves out right in the midst of worship. When the people of God come together in worship, I tell you the truth, look out and expect God to show up. Because of His obedience in worship, Jehoshaphat received double. Talk about a real transference of wealth. Man, that boy had so many goods to collect; he collected goods for three days.

It does not matter how hard or gruesome your adversity is; God is able. Focus your eyes on Jesus and direct your attention on Him. He will! I said He will work turn it around for you and those you are praying for. God asked Abraham "Is there anything too hard for God? The answer…Nothing! Jesus loves you so much. Daughter and son, I declare to you today that you will survive, you will get through this and surely you will overcome. You are coming out more than a conqueror.

> The fear of God came upon all the kingdoms of the countries when they heard how the Lord had fought against the enemies of Israel. And the kingdom of Jehoshaphat was at peace, for his God had given him rest on every side.
> —2 Chronicles 20:30

Rest on Every Side

Rest on every side can be yours. In the midst of adversity we can choose as did Jehoshaphat to set our eyes on the Lord. In spite of the vast army, in spite of the negative news the doctor has delivered. In spite of losing your job, and when your finances are over your head. In spite of your child facing a serious illness. In spite of the death of a loved one. In spite of a broken marriage that resulted in divorce. In spite of suffering from abuse and emotional bondage, you will receive victory on every side. Choose to make God your pursuit and set your eyes on Him.

Inquire of the Lord and receive that word of hope, healing, and victory in your life today. His grace is sufficient to see you through to victory. Total victory! Not just survival, but total victory!

Discipline or the Devil

God disciplines those He loves. Sometimes my little girl carries on with tantrums when she's disciplined or corrected. And boy does her whining get ugly. Not every trial or adversity is what it appears. In other words, not all setbacks are the Devil's work. Oftentimes the Lord will allow us to go through correction that we may be able to stand as we grow and cover new ground. Pressure and correction is good for us in building our character and bringing us to maturity.

I would say to my princess that I love you and want the best for you. I want to see you growing strong and healthy with plausible habits and a strong character. I would sit with her, having a heart to heart to insure that she understands my discipline. Princess, I correct you to help you, not to hurt you. According to her, she would respond,

"You are hurting my feelings." Well! Correction hurts sometimes, and like medicine, it tastes real bad, but it's for your good. It fights off the bad stuff in our character, just as medicine fights off germs, bacteria, and foreign agents in our bodies. Correction, like medicine, helps you to recover and gain new strength.

In a classroom setting, we must take correction, humble ourselves, and receive instruction. Otherwise we will never get it right or learn. Receive correction, learn from it, and conquer the problem, that you may move to the next level. When we call on God seeking answers, it is important that we wait in receiving His instructions.

Habakkuk's Complaint

In a world of injustices where it seems that the wicked go unpunished or others get away with murder, fret not yourself. God sees and God knows. There is nothing that goes unnoticed in His sight. Habakkuk asked questions and brought his complaint to the Lord when he was troubled. After receiving God's answer, he responded with a prayer of faith. This is where many of us fail. We receive an answer from God, but continue to whine, trip, and complain over the situation.

When your adversities become unbearable look up to God and patiently wait on His timing. For in time you will receive the answer if you hang in there. As you struggle and face calamity, Habakkuk's example is one that should encourage you to move from doubt to faith and in the process, wait on the Lord. He encouraged himself that even in times of loss, famine, and drought, he would rejoice in the Lord. His outlook was not based on the events that surrounded him, but by faith in God's ability to strengthen him and see about him.

> Though the fig tree does not bud and there are no grapes on the vine, though the olive crop fails and the fields produce no food, though there are no sheep in the pen and no cattle in the stalls, yet I will rejoice in the LORD, I will be joyful in God my Savior.
> The Sovereign LORD is my strength, He makes my feet like the feet of a deer, He enables me to go on the heights.
> —Habakkuk 3:17–19

Instead of looking at the calamity, blaming others and the devil, look to God and press into Him. Habakkuk was determined to keep his focus and trust in the Lord. Accept God's discipline and timing. Ask Him to help you change. Ultimately the purpose of discipline and correction is for you to change.

See your oppositions as stepping-stones to place you in the right position. Our struggles are beneficial in that they build us, develop us, redirect us, and sometimes bring out of us untapped potentials. As you are faced with setbacks, turn your face toward God and bless His name. Thank Him that this, too, will pass. Thank Him that your sun will shine again.

However dark your situation, morning must come. The sun must shine again. Wrongs or adversities will not last forever. God says to you hold on to the vision. It will surely come. You will surely overcome.

My friend, lift up your eyes to hills from whence cometh your help. You will not fall in a time when many are falling. You will stand and declare the work of the Lord and it will be marvelous in your sight. Push into His presence until there's daybreak and once daybreak comes take your worship to the next level. Let your worship to the King transition you to heights unknown. Say to yourself that your worship will not be driven by what you see or what God can do for you, but by pure love, faith, and adoration of who He is. He is love and He will enable you to go on to the heights.

THE SETUP FOR THE COMEBACK

PRAYER

Father, in Jesus' name I pray for Your daughter and son today. I specifically pray for those who are pressing on in spite of the storm. I pray for those whose hope and trust is in You. I also speak an encouraging word to their very spirits that they will live and not die. You shall obtain gladness and joy. Take up your position and watch the Lord deliver. O God, I pray all of heaven would descend right now, this very moment and surround them with power from on high. Strengthen Your servant and give them victory on every side. I pray Your peace that passes all understanding will guard their very hearts. Right now in the name of Jesus the forces of darkness, spiritual wickedness, principalities and powers are dismantled and are rendered powerless over your lives. In Jesus' name.

Now my friend, receive His love and worship Him.

Chapter Eight

HEALING AND RESTORATION ARE YOURS

AT MY NEW place, I had gone through a period of nightmares and oppression. I had difficulty shaking them off so I once again resolved to turn my eyes to the Lord in much fasting and praying. During that time something significant happened: For the first time in years, I felt a peace that no man could give. That prayer broke an unforgiveness that remained in me that I was completely blinded to. I finally forgave all that contributed to the horrid sexual abuse that tormented me for years.

I've forgiven and I've been forgiven. Oh, what a relief! Truly to whom much is given much is required. It's amazing how we unconsciously hold on to pain and unforgiveness. We busy ourselves with work and kingdom ministry never addressing the root of our pain or our hang-ups. In turn we repeat a cycle of oppression until like a runaway train we face a spiritual collision or breakdown.

You may have found yourself in a place of no return. The pain of the past, the shame of what you've done or who you've become has you so bound that you've resorted to accept it as "It is what it is." It is never too late! God hasn't given up on you so why are you giving up on God? Remember that He is love. His love covers you further than you could ever imagine. His desire and plan is to give you a hope and future. He wants you to live life in abundance. I know that the pain and shame can be overwhelmingly too much for us to handle. With God all things are possible and in His presence, He will wipe away your tears. He will remove your pain and He will drive back every force of bondage that seeks to rob you of the liberty Christ has given. Healing and restoration is assuredly yours when you find yourself at His feet. Have a heart-to-heart with God. There is nothing hidden from Him. He knows all about you and is waiting for you to accept His invitation. My friend, come to Jesus just as you are. He's not asking you to clean up your act, correct your fault, and then come. He is calling you just as you are. Give it all to Him. The pain, the shame, and the struggle—we must give Him everything. Whatever the secret struggle or pain is, no longer run or hide the very thing that God wants to heal. Remember that when you come to God in worship, His love covers you. He will draw you to Himself and deliver you from yourself as you become a reflection of His love. God wants you whole and complete.

When faced with pressure or adversity, it is extremely important that we not rush the process, hurdle over the process, or bury the process. We must go through it, confront it, and overcome it. When a bad wound or sore is ignored it will either grow worse with time or remain a sore. Like a slipped disk in your back, no matter how much you take an adjustment it will slip again and again with one wrong move. The corrective measure was never applied, only a temporary solution. Therefore, healing becomes temporary. The healing never penetrated to the root, just the surface was covered. This kind of healing is incomplete and it will sooner or later create a deeper and more dangerous wound. Instead of colliding like a freight train, choose to run into His presence and be freed from all hurt, struggle, and adversity.

We have a tendency to pray or get in His presence when trouble comes or some level of distress arises. We run to the doctor when a problem arises and receive a temporary solution. The permanent solution would be to get to the root of the problem and administer the corrective measures. In the same manner, we should not enter into His presence for a temporary fix. His presence should be our way of life. In His presence there is fullness of all that God is, but our worship should not focus on the fullness or splendor or temporary fix. Our worship should be directed to God because our love and devotion to Him is pure, broken, and sincere with no strings attached. Your worship should go forth as "God this is beyond me, I've tried and just can't stop. I want to be whole and I want to be restored. Please Lord, help me." When you pray like that and you are sincere, get ready for transformation. This kind of worship will tug at His heart every time and in turn you will enjoy the benefits of His splendor and Kingdom. In His presence, we can enjoy more than a temporary fix. We will experience the joy of the Lord and all the fullness that comes with Him. Your life will be transformed and healing will be complete.

Sincere Worship Gets His Attention

I've learned that worship humbles the heart. Pride can never stand in the face of God's worship. Total healing and restoration requires our worship to be broken. Even in serving or doing the simple things, we are giving God His worth. Because we love Him, we serve Him and it is important that we do it truthfully, joyfully, and willingly.

> "God is a Spirit and those that worship Him must worship Him in spirit and in truth."
> —John 4:24

An honest worship will always get the attention of God. He is not looking for something false or attractive in words and formality. God seeks for something that is broken. When we realize that in ourselves we are incapable and that no degree, social status, or royal heir from our history has the power to sustain us; and only God can deliver, then we are broken. This is how we ought to come before the Lord: We come knowing that He is our deliverer, helper, comforter, and healer.

> The sacrifices of God are a broken spirit, a broken and contrite heart . . . these, O God, you will not despise.
> —Psalm 51:17

We must allow ourselves to be forgiven and healed from past and present failures, hurts, and oppressions. Never conquering your adversity will give it room to come back to haunt you. You must put your foot on the neck of every adversity or it will show its face again. This was something I learned later on in life.

Though I survived abuse and sickness, setbacks and failures, they were never dethroned, dismantled, annihilated. Future adversities caused me to realize that I must bring to an end by the power of God every enemy and opposition that sets out to destroy or distract me. I must overcome and conquer before I can truly advance. I must deal with my struggles, conquer them once and for all, and live the life of an overcomer.

Favor Flows When We Worship

Total deliverance, healing, divine cancellation of debts, and divine acceleration can be yours.

Liberation from any kind of bondage, taskmaster, or oppression over your life can be yours because of the Lord's grace and favor.

In having such favor, friendship with God is vital. The key to receiving is always delighting ourselves in the Lord. Growing in favor with God hinges on our intense pursuit of Him. When God sees our determination to chase after Him with all our heart, He releases an anointing to proclaim favor and vindication. (See Isaiah 61).

In the anointing of Christ we can proclaim "favor" and set into motion, like the laws of gravity, a power that causes everything in our lives to come into divine order. What goes up must come down. When we send up to God our all—our love, our appreciation, the setbacks, and the adversities—He shows up with all that He is in power and glory. With God on the scene intervention is inevitable and victory is imminent.

In His presence an anointing to overcome and obtain victory is released on us that we can call heaven's court into session and call the heavenly host to be our witness. Wherever there is injustice, sickness, disease, death, poverty, bondage, oppression, and false accusations we can declare vindication. We can declare the provision and favor of God to overtake every injustice. For Jesus promised He will give His angels charge over us. When adversities come against us the Spirit of the Lord will raise up a standard against it. And that standard is that the gates of hell will not prevail against any of His beloved.

HEALING AND RESTORATION ARE YOURS

PRAYER

Father, in Jesus' name I pray for Your daughter and son today. I specifically pray for those that are broken before You. Thank You Lord that they have made You their everything. I also pray that in the midst of their pursuit of You, they will continually experience Your healing power. O God, I pray all of heaven would descend right now, this very moment and surround them with power from on high. Above all else, I pray that they will never go back to Egypt but they will advance to their promised land and occupy. I pray victory over every enemy. I declare that Jesus, You are resuscitating that which was dead and making them new again. Right now in the name of Jesus the forces of darkness and every setback over their lives are rendered powerless. The Lord rebuke you, foul spirit of besiegement; release this daughter, release this son right now in Jesus' name.

Now my friend, receive His love and worship Him.

Chapter Nine

SETBACKS ARE NOT FINAL

WELL! IT'S THE life of a married woman. Married and have children, busy, busy, busy. Children have me busy, husband has me busy (real busy) but not what you're thinking. Ministry has me busy. Child bearing wasn't easy. Delivery of both my children almost ended in death. In my second pregnancy I carried twins and lost one child; however, after a few days I had developed a severe infection and carried a fever of 107.5 degrees.

During fellowship, with the saints at my bedside, the fever intensified suddenly right after breaking bread (the Lord's Supper). I took a short nap, got out of bed feeling real weak and feverish and called out for help. Please take me to the hospital *now*! I felt something was very wrong. After praying and arriving at the hospital I smelled a strange stench of death surrounding me. God works in mysterious ways, I tell you. If not for that smell I believe they (the doctors) would have killed me. During delivery I had had a cesarean so they automatically assumed the incision was infected. Due to its urgency, they pried me opened without medication. (My God, did it hurt!) They squeezed and squeezed searching for inflammation, but there was none. When they realized the smell was inside the womb they proceeded with the proper treatment. It turned out that the infection was in my womb and it was a miracle that I didn't die. Apparently this infection was lurking in the dark and intended to take me out, but God!

Before my first child was born, I was diagnosed with multiple sclerosis. The doctors claimed that I would lose mobility of my limbs and would eventually be confined to a wheelchair. (The Devil is a liar.) The myelin tissue was rapidly deteriorating and the cerebellum showed multiple scars and inflammation. They said there was nothing else they could do other than administer pain management. I declared daily, "I will live and not die." "I will declare the work of the Lord," I said. "This setback will be to the glory of God and I will testify of His awesome healing power."

Things became very difficult at this point of my life. I was now taking new ground in ministry and knew that the call of God and anointing rested upon me heavily to evangelize and to declare His work. I couldn't understand this opposition and apparent setback. My body often rocked in pain and my ability to walk straight and hold objects diminished.

"God, I know that you didn't bring me this far to leave me," I prayed. "I shall not die, but live" became my everyday confession. My eyes remained on Jesus. And my trust was in Him alone. I reminded myself that Jesus is my healer. He will take care of me and this, too, shall pass.

Stand On His Word

Discouragement laid upon me so heavily that all I could do was resolve to prayer and fasting. I refused to be overcome by the appearance of the setbacks. All I knew was that Jesus had said I am healed; so in spite of how I felt I was determined. "I won't let go, Lord." My change, my healing, and my breakthrough will come. It will happen, and God will be glorified.

God's Word is true and He will not fail. We must be determined to hold on to His promises no matter what. He is more than able to do the impossible. There is no situation, sickness, or disease that He cannot turn around, heal, or repair. He is able!

Everyone in my network joined with me in prayer and fasting and we believed God for a miracle. I know that He will do it. He's done it before and He will do it again. We must never use the word *defeat*. Stand on the promises of God and claim every one of them. God is not a man that He should lie; neither is He the son of man that He should repent. What he has ordained He will maintain. When God says let

EXPECT THE UNEXPECTED

there be, there must be. By His stripes I am healed! He will do it again. I trust Him.

Well! In short after several visits to the doctor and after numerous testings and medication for pain management, I was miraculously healed and cleared from multiple sclerosis. According to the doctors some unusual phenomenon occurred and there's got to be an explanation, "remission" they called it. Yet they could not explain the disappearances of the scars, inflammation, and deteriorated myelin tissue. I told them that it's *all* Jesus. His name is *Jesus*!! He has touched me and made me whole.

I requested them to recheck every exam and when the results came back, they were left speechless, fully amazed at my recovery and the miraculous transformation. It was all gone; there was no inflammation of the brain, no scarred tissue and the myelin was fully repaired. Hallelujah! I was completely healed. At the name of Jesus every knee shall bow and every tongue confess that Jesus is Lord to the glory of God the Father. Not a trace of ever having suffered from multiple sclerosis remained in my body; there were just medical notes and the doctors couldn't explain it. Ha ha! Jesus is my portion, my healer, and my reward!

Years later my thyroid went haywire and overactive causing Graves Disease, which almost killed me suddenly. Everything in my body skyrocketed, causing near fatal readings. By divine intervention, God stepped in and delivered. He's always on time. Through intense prayer with my family and loved ones, we believed God for a miracle. A miracle I received. Again, Jesus is my portion, my healer, and my reward.

Press Forward and Complete the Task

Sometimes in life, we may face challenges that appear impossible. The race or task may appear insurmountable, but to the one that commits to complete it, you shall overcome. At times in life we are heavy laden with much to do and no help in sight. Resources are limited and so much is against us rather than for us. This was how Zerubbabel felt when he and the exiles returned to Babylon. Upon returning, they set about on the large task of rebuilding the temple.

In the beginning they were full with zeal, ready to take on anything. Yes, we can do this. Excited about the vision and moving forward, their enthusiasm began to wane as obstacles in accomplishing the task came into focus. Furthermore, their resources became limited and opposition from the Samaritans didn't make it any easier. Does this kind of situation sound familiar to you? Moving forward in spite of the pressures only to face more resistance? I know this feeling very well and if not careful to cast it upon the Lord, it will overwhelm you.

All these things brought discouragement among them. They began to lose hope and at that low point, received an encouraging word from the prophet Zechariah. Sometimes all we need is just one word. At the right moment that word has the power to lift you or destroy you. Be mindful of what you say because you never really know where someone stands in their inner man in the midst of crisis. They could very well be hanging on to dear life and your words could change their situation for better or worse.

> "This is the word of the Lord to Zerubbabel: 'Not by might nor by power, but by My Spirit,' says the Lord Almighty. What are you, O mighty mountain? Before Zerubbabel you will become level ground. Then he will bring out the capstone to shouts of 'God bless it! God bless it!' Then the word of the Lord came to me: 'The hands of Zerubbabel have laid the foundation of this temple; His hands will also complete it. Then you will know that the Lord Almighty has sent me to you.'"
> —Zechariah 4:6–9

It is not by human strength or power that the battle would be won. Not by human intelligence or strategy, but by His Spirit. In the face of discouragement your strength or own intervention will never bring the victory. Victory will come forth when we rely on the Lord in total worship and abandonment of our self-efforts, saying, "God I cannot do this, it is by your Spirit." I will sing and I will shout, "God bless it! God favor it! Let His power, authority and favor do the work." The challenge may look impossible, but His grace is sufficient.

My God is able and He will do it. You will bring this temple to completion not by human power or engineering ability. When you open your mouth and declare God's ability and greatness, you will complete the task and finish it. It shall be done and the Lord will bless it. Calling those things that are not as though they were. The Lord will bless it.

Principle of Metamorphosis

Destiny is a process. To live is to grow, to grow is to change, to change is to be transformed. Transformation is to change from one form to another. Therefore, spiritual growth denotes change after change, after change. God is changing me and He's changing you. In worship, we will be transformed and delivered from ourselves.

During the process of metamorphosis the caterpillar (low place) is transformed into a butterfly (place to soar). The butterfly soars and pollinates plants and flowers causing them to reproduce. This is somewhat like evangelism. We share the gospel and God's love pollinating the earth with His goodness and reproduce believers, making disciples.

There are two stages that bring about metamorphosis:

- Caterpillar—At this stage the caterpillar receives life; it eats, grows, and sheds its skin.
- Cocoon—This stage is the chamber of change. The caterpillar goes through a transforming process; it's boxed in, and is enclosed,

pressed on every side. It is transformed from one form to another: the caterpillar dies and the butterfly lives.

Just as the caterpillar receives life, we receive life when we receive the Lord as our personal Savior. We are born again; and our transformation doesn't stop there. We grow by studying God's Word and learning how to trust Him. Through many trials we prove His promises and live out His promises by eating on the Word of God and we begin to shed our sinful skin. And so our transformation begins.

In the cocoon, we approach and face many dark situations, trials, testings, and adversities. We are no longer in our comfort zone. At this stage, the caterpillar dies in the cocoon and prepares for a new life.

In the cocoon of our lives, we must be careful to die the right kind of death. We should become dead to sin, but alive to Christ. Dying to the fleshly reactions of our adversities—unaffected by them and victorious in spite of them.

In adverse situations, we sometimes claim, "O, thank God for my salvation. . . . "If I wasn't saved, man . . . I would blank, blank. . ." It's not enough to just walk away from an ugly situation. We must conquer it by showing God's love, patience, kindness, and forgiveness. The cocoon is there to kill the ugliness in you. God wants to eradicate the fleshly, heartless you and transform you into a reflection of

His beauty. God is not trying to change the situation, but He is changing you.

Your past may look pretty dark because of choices you've made and choices you haven't made. Don't lose hope, there's life and light ahead of you. It's not over and you will live. There is life after failure. There is life after imprisonment. There is life after the cocoon.

People may try to permanently stamp your ugliness on you and try to keep you boxed in. The Enemy would be satisfied knowing that you've chosen to remain in the cocoon. I declare that, like the caterpillar, you will break out of the mold, spread your wings, and soar.

Realize that if someone helps the butterfly out of the cocoon, its wings will not develop and it will not be able to fly. It will soon die. Don't try to escape the cocoon by other means other than the Lord Himself. Only His ways are perfect and only His power and help is eternal. So with the help of the Lord via your devotion and worship to Him; spread your wings and fly, butterfly, fly.

It's Time to Soar

Raise up your hands in worship and soar. In your struggle or cocoon, don't fight or praise for victory but worship and praise from the place of victory for the warfare is accomplished. It's already done and the victory is already yours.

Let the weak say, "I am strong!" Open your mouth and shout, "Victory!" With eagle's' wings you will never come down. Conquer, subdue, pollinate, reproduce, and let His glory fill the earth! Get in His presence and worship.

Anytime you are faced with a flood of trials and adversities, know that there is divine purpose on your life and you are about to bust out of the mold, the cocoon. The Enemy is scared and attempts to snuff you out. The Devil would like to have a party knowing that he stole your voice, your praise, and your worship.

Oh, but I declare that it won't work. You are who God says you are. You can do what God says you can do. There is a sword in your mouth and you will not use it against yourself by speaking defeat. You will shout in the face of adversity and obtain healing. You will obtain victory and soar.

This metamorphosis is good for you. Say to your cocoon, "You ain't seen nothing yet." I declare that you will come out. Say it: "I am coming out!" Like that butterfly coming from a caterpillar (low place), you are spreading your wings. Let Jesus be your all in all. Trust Him, love Him, seek Him, and walk with Him—and soar with Him.

Backed Against the Wall

The most trying time of my adult life has been this current period. Understand that in the midst of the storm God is moving. Great things are happening right before my very eyes. Opportunities for ministry are being extended around me and I'm experiencing growth. I'm enjoying the pastorate of serving the body, teaching the Word and seeing lives transformed.

In the midst of all the success there are pressures all around. Who can I call on but the Lord? Everyone turns to me for answers, prayers, and help when I need help myself. Recently I almost came to a place where I thought I would lose my mind. I became emotionally numb due to family pressures, depression, deaths, and various setbacks.

I went to my physician and broke down in tears, but of course he couldn't help me. It was so difficult to hold the fort when my own life needed support to be upheld. Imagine a foundation pillar holding up a structure. The pillar has cracks and is under immense pressure. Will it hold? Or will it break? When I thought it couldn't get worse, it did. Home and family were pressured on every side and my heart ached beyond human repair. Within months, I lost a dear mother in the gospel at a time I most needed her. This was a colossal ache and oh, how much I miss her with each passing day.

I felt so empty and alone. I cried without end, as it seemed. It felt as though my insides were being torn apart. My inner being ached and words could not express it. My secret, you know—I worshipped my way through to face each new day. Every breath and new day came by the strengthening of the Lord. In addition to this my finances became limited and I was under extreme pressure with emotional stresses and unresolved matters that caused me to break down further.

Don't Break Under the Pressure

At my breaking point I just wanted to find a cave and hide from it all, ministry, church, family, and everything. It felt like my mind was going. Oh, but Jesus—I love the Lord so passionately and couldn't bear the thought of not having Him in my life. My secret? Worship. I again resolved to sincere and intense prayer and fasting (my life depended on it) and I heard the voice of God say, "Move to Georgia." In my mind I responded, how would this solve my problems? I can't just move. Why Georgia? Where will I stay? Where will I live?

I was busy working a pastorate and directing an outreach program. How will I get out of this? I thought to myself. How could I leave the church, the outreach, everything I was doing and all that I put my life into? Oh, dear God, how?

This was exponentially one of the hardest things I've had to do, in spite of the pressures I was faced with. Oh, the thoughts that ran through my mind. What will I tell the congregation? What will they say? How will I tell them? What about my family? What about my finances? The questions went on. The Lord so lovingly responded while I was in prayer, "My daughter, I love you so much more than you can imagine. You are concerned over things that need not concern you. Remember it is all mine. Do not be dismayed, neither be afraid, for I am with you. You are my beloved. Reposition yourself, stand firm and see what I will do.

I moved to Georgia, an unfamiliar place and new environment No friends and familiar faces, no job, and no money. My thoughts were, God, you must be up to something real good because looking with the natural eye this just doesn't make sense. My life has always been one of faith. Trusting God for everything in every way. I arrived in Georgia not fully knowing what my next move would be. I stayed with my children at a sister's house for one week exact. I spent the entire week in prayer. Before the week ended, the Spirit of the Lord prompted me to get up and start looking for an apartment.

I said, "Father, I have no income and it is not feasible for me to afford rent, much less function with the current overwhelming oppositions of monumental crisis, emotional breakdowns, family discord, dysfunction, and a wounded heart. However, I know that you are in control and I am obeying your voice."

He whispered, "Watch me Baby Girl, watch me."

Fast, Pray, and Expect God to Move

I continued to wait on the Lord in fasting and prayer. Throughout my life, I have proven this to work. My favorite motto is "A life of prayer and consecration is preparation for a dynamic demonstration of Kingdom administration." Through my life of prayer and fasting I have proven God to move supernaturally again and again.

Fasting and praying is good, but we must remember that trusting God and expecting Him to move is just as important. One should not resort to fasting and praying as a last resort. It should become a lifestyle.

Many are the afflictions of the righteous, but the Lord will deliver us from them all. It is through Him and by Him all things are permitted and destroyed. The Devil never has the final say-so over our lives. Remember that the Enemy's power is only suggestive and the end result is up to the choice we make. Will we seek the Lord or will we wallow in our mess?

The Bible states that after Solomon finished building the temple, the Lord appeared to him with this promise:

> When I shut up the heavens so that there is no rain, or command locusts to devour the land or send plague among my people, if my people, who are called by name will humble themselves and pray and seek my face and turn form their wicked ways, then will I hear from heaven and will forgive their sins and will heal their land."
> —2 Chronicles 7:13-14

Though fasting and praying should be a way of life as a believer, there are times when we must specifically call a fast to break the strongholds of darkness. Let us follow the examples of various Bible-time leaders who called upon the Lord in the day of adversity and expected the supernatural intervention of God. Be reminded that we ought not

SETBACKS ARE NOT FINAL

to live by bread alone, but by God's Word. Live and stand on all of His promises.

Jesus said, "Watch and pray so that you will not fall into temptation. The spirit is willing, but the body is weak" (Matthew 26:41). When you pray, when you fast, and when you worship, do them expecting God to respond. Just as worship delivers us from ourselves, I believe that fasting carries a similar effect. We are saying to God, "Not my will, Lord, but your will be done. I must decrease that you may increase."

The flesh is indeed weak. In our flesh we are quick to doubt and we automatically think the worst in the face of adversity. For example: Your loved one is traveling on a certain highway and there has been a fatal car accident; automatically our heart races and we think, oh, God! In our flesh, we will always take the easy, passive, or lesser route. But by the Spirit of God we gear up with new zest, stamina, boldness, courage, and aggression that says, *"Live!* I shall live and not die! I will not entertain seeds of defeat and negativity. I will lift up my eyes to the King, who is my everything.

The Father's desire for us exceeds our own thoughts and imaginations. For truly eyes have not seen and ears have not heard the wonderful things God has in store for us, except through the Spirit. We must learn to rest in His promises and expect the best and expect victory every time. We must learn to trust in the Lord with all our hearts. Never move according to our own understanding, but lean on Jesus, seek Him and trust Him always.

When God Gives a Vision He Makes Provision

After much prayer and obeying the Lord to venture out and search for an apartment, in the span of one day I began my search and filled out some applications. Later in the evening of the next day, I was approved for a two-bedroom two-bath luxury apartment after being turned down for the lesser appealing affordable ones. Keep in mind I had no job and no money. I said again, "Father, you know that I cannot afford this and although the natural thing would be that I should not get approval for this . . . you do all things well and I thank you for all you are doing and will do."

I remained at peace and followed in obedience. Somehow, some way, God miraculously and speedily moved on my behalf. Within seven days of moving to Georgia with no money and no furniture, I moved into my beautiful apartment and month after month the Lord miraculously and supernaturally provided rent, utilities, car payment, and food. The finances and provision just kept on coming. In the meantime I remained busy about the Lord's work.

Prayer

Father, in Jesus' name I pray for Your daughter and son today. I specifically pray for those that are faced with sudden setbacks in their pursuit of You. Father, endow them with new strength and new stamina. I also pray that You will bear them up on eagle's wings and cause them to soar against the winds of adversity. O God, I pray all of heaven would descend right now, this very moment and surround them with power from on high. Above all else, I pray that every setback will be used as an instrument to catapult them straight to victory. They will experience right now Your favor and provision in every area of need. Advance them, Lord Jesus, and bless them with an overwhelming flood of Your favor. The Lord rebuke you, foul spirit of accusation; release this daughter, release this son right now in Jesus' name.

Now my friend, receive His love and worship Him.

Chapter Ten

ENOUGH IS ENOUGH!

DIRECTED BY THE Holy Spirit, I formed a community Bible study and held a community outreach revival where souls were saved, ministered to, and transformed. The Lord backed up this venture and every need was met for the financing. I helped wherever help was needed. The blessings kept on coming and God miraculously provided all my personal and financial needs.

God never gives a vision without making provision. He backs it up satisfaction guaranteed and never leaves you empty-handed. I often say, "Saints, we are blessed to be a blessing." Give and it will come back.

The blessing will come when we selflessly put out. Our setbacks may discourage us or cause us to lose sight but be encouraged to stay focused. Don't be swayed by the appearance of lack. Setbacks are just setups to be used as stepping-stones to take us to our next level. Hold strong to faith and walk in obedience the best you know how and God does the rest. Truly little becomes much when we leave it in the Master's hand.

During this season I was again faced with news from the doctor. After a series of painful abdominal pains, I was rushed to the emergency room and the physicians discovered four masses in my body. One of them raised a serious concern. They said it was my pancreas. The doctor stated that it could be malignant and it is an organ that they do not want to touch. Touching it could end with fatal results. Oh, but there is a Doctor who knows this frame! Matter of fact, He created it and His name is Jesus. The chief Physician and Surgeon. Nothing is too difficult for Him. Is there anything too hard for God? Nothing, absolutely nothing!

Shout in the Face of Adversity

The Enemy wants to steal your voice. Sometimes we have to open our mouths in worship and declare what says the Lord. Your words and declaration bring about change. When you speak "let there be" there *will be*, because you defined it. I once heard a preacher say that God listens to the tone of your voice. I put it this way: How bad do you want it? As stated before, it's not about the storm but it's about how you react to the storm. Say to your circumstance, "I will not be silent." You will praise your way through and will shout life and call every darkness light. Choose to stop praying to God about how big your problem is and start telling your problem how great your God is.

At this point I became angry at the Devil. I was tired of sickness. I was tired of the hospital. Tired of needles and all the poking. A holy anger came upon me. I was sick of being sick. Enough is enough! This sickness is not unto death, but for the glory of God. I am the righteousness of God. My body is the temple of the Lord. I will not just exist and take this beating. By His stripes I am healed. Throughout my life, I've experienced healing and witnessed many being healed. I am healed and this is the last time!

After my brief moment of discouragement, I went to pray; with fervency and authority I shouted out with tears running down. Enough is enough! The kingdom of God suffereth violence and the violent take it by force. I was reminded of Nahum 1:9, "affliction shall not rise up the second time."

> The LORD is good, a refuge in times of trouble. He cares for those who trust in him, but with an overwhelming flood he will make an end of Nineveh; he will pursue his foes into darkness.
> Whatever they plot against the LORD he will bring to an end; trouble will not come a second time.
> —Nahum 1:7–9

I declared to my body, "This is the last time. It stops here. No more torment, no more afflictions, no more sickness, no more barrenness, and no more lack. *It is finished*! This attack on my body has to stop, it is finished and by His stripes *I am healed!*"

Put Your Foot on the Neck of Every Enemy

I will not be defeated. I will not be discouraged. I will survive and I will overcome and conquer every battle, every enemy, every foe, every adversity, and every struggle. Joshua discovered this secret to not only survive but also overcome and destroy every enemy.

Joshua was commanded to destroy the five kings that hid in the cave at Makkedah and put them under his feet. The Enemy belongs under our feet. Jesus said that He has given us power to walk over serpents and scorpions and over all the power of the Enemy.

I once heard a fellow laborer in the gospel say that our circumstances are like the mattress we sleep on. You cannot sleep under the mattress. Your outlook should never be "Well, under the circumstances I'm doing OK." Why are you under your circumstances? Resting under the circumstances or mattress will suffocate you. However, if we sleep above it, on top of it, our sleep will be more restful.

If your adversities are over you, they will suffocate you and eventually kill you. But when we place those adversities under our feet, we can rest and live in the peace that God gives. When trouble arises, rest on the promises of Jesus and take your attention off the problem.

Adversities, enemies, setbacks, trials, and struggles are, in a nutshell, distractions to take our focus off the Lord. They are suggestions that will steal our worship to God if we don't eradicate them. When Joshua fought the battle at Jericho, He received victory and conquered many enemies. He had set out to destroy every foe and opposition that came against him. However, a few enemies (the five kings of the Amorites) who had joined forces to destroy the Gibeonites fled the scene in fear of being annihilated by Joshua's army. The five kings survived and took cover, but God wasn't through just yet. Joshua received word that they were hiding and he sent word to trap them. He understood that if you don't clean up the sore that causes infection, it will sooner or later return to haunt you. Let's look at the five kings of the Amorites from the Bible that represent distractions simply put and let us learn this lesson from Joshua that we ought to destroy strongholds once and for all.

- King of Jerusalem—represents oppression (keeps you in bondage).
- King of Hebron—represents religion (form of godliness).
- King of Jarmuth—represents besiegement (thief).
- King of Lachish—represents blindness (lack of knowledge).

- King of Eglon—represents accusations (accuser of the brethren).

These five kings joined forces and set out to destroy the children of God. Today in our individual lives these kinds of demonic forces still show their faces, seeking to rob us of total victory. Oppression, religion, besiegement, blindness, and accusations come in many faces and cripple us from advancing. They must be eradicated and placed under our feet.

It is the Spirit of the Lord that will destroy these demonic strongholds and we must resolve to stay on our faces in consecration and worship to the Lord. In doing so we have power not just to shut them up, but to destroy them and place our feet upon their necks. They are rendered powerless as we set ourselves to worship and focus our eyes on Jesus.

> The LORD said to Joshua, "Do not be afraid of them; I have given them into your hand. Not one of them will be able to withstand you."
> —Joshua 10:8

My friend, not one of your enemies will be able to stand against you. But you will refute them, subdue them and render them powerless.

> On the day the LORD gave the Amorites over to Israel, Joshua said to the LORD in the presence of Israel, "O sun, stand still over Gibeon, O moon, over the Valley of Aijalon."

> So the sun stood still and the moon stopped, till the nation avenged itself on its enemies. . . .
>
> The sun stopped in the middle of the sky and delayed going down about a full day. There has never been a day like it before or since, a day when the LORD listened to a man.
> —Joshua 10:12–14

As said before, when we worship the King of Kings, He will skip over millions just to come see about us. God listens when we worship. We get His attention when we call upon Him in worship, adoration, and love. Imagine, God allowed the sun to stop so that His children can receive victory, increase and experience the overflow from their adversities. Wow!

As you conquer your enemies, it's not by might nor by power but by the Spirit of the Lord. Your worship will transcend all of heaven to your realm. And where God shows up, all of darkness will be destroyed. Don't allow your struggles to remain, but take them out completely. Don't stop at surviving the storm, eradicate the storm and it won't come back. The Lord further said:

> But don't stop! Pursue your enemies, attack them from the rear and don't let them reach their cities, for the LORD your God has given them into your hand. So Joshua and the Israelites destroyed them completely.
> —Joshua 10:19, 20

Joshua then spoke to the army commanders:

> "Come here and put your feet on the necks of these kings. . . . Do not be afraid, do not be discouraged. Be strong and courageous. This is what the LORD will do to all the enemies you are going to fight.'"
>
> Joshua 10:24, 25

Do not be afraid, and do not be discouraged. But be strong and courageous for the battle is not yours but belongs to the Lord. Just has the Lord did for David, Jehoshaphat, Israel, Joshua, Zerubbabel, Habakkuk, Paul, and Silas, He will do for you. Model their life of worship and see what the Lord will do to every enemy that comes against you. As you make the Lord your pursuit and set your eyes to worship Him, you will survive and you will overcome.

> "But for you who revere my name, the sun of righteousness will rise with healing in its wings. And you will go out and leap like calves released from the stall. Then you will trample down the wicked; they will be ashes under the soles of your feet on the day when I do these things," says the LORD Almighty.
>
> —Malachi 4:2–3

To those who give reverence and worship to the Lord, you will go forth with power and victory. You will trample under your feet every force of darkness and wickedness. You will bring them down to nothing as declared in the Word of God.

Throughout all the adversities of my life, God is still on the throne. I am determined to continuously advance and occupy. Shortly after living in the apartment, I felt led to start looking into purchasing a house. By this time, I obtained ridiculous faith and trusted God to work it out. I needed more space and so did my children.

In short, God supernaturally delivered. Within eight months of coming to Georgia, I moved into my beautiful brand new five-bedroom home. And it is gorgeous. It was the Lord! He provided every financial need, and gave me favor upon favor. According to man's outlook, this was not and is not possible. Especially during this time of economic distress and the struggling financial market, my progresses were beyond man's doing and ability. But God always makes the impossible possible. Our worship draws us close to the Father and He in turn draws nearer. In His presence there is life, victory, and the ability to live above the seeming distractions and oppositions that threaten our existence. The favor of God will open doors that no man can shut. Favor will connect you with all the right connections, restoring and releasing supernatural breakthroughs and provision. Through many tears and pain, heartbreaks and trials. Through sickness, grief, financial setbacks, possessions lost and family dysfunction; God has certainly walked with me, better yet carried me. Through it all, God has delivered on all occasion an unexpected, unlikely and extra-ordinary victory and breakthroughs. The traumas, setbacks, and oppositions encountered did not make me a product of abuse or defeat. I boldly proclaim that greater is Jesus in me than he that is in the world. Yes, I am stronger, yes I am better, yes I am wiser and the best is still yet to come! When God shows up, He shows up on a grand scale. Hallelujah! The Lord has healed. The Lord has delivered. The Lord has given the victory. And it is marvelous in my sight.

By faith and by His grace I am completely healed, restored, and living as an overcomer. Though adversities come, I will overcome in spite of them. I am determined to make the Lord my every pursuit. For He is my source, the very air I breathe. He is the lover of my soul. My passion and my pursuit.

Right now, if you are faced with adversities and find yourself stuck, it is time to advance and come out from your place of struggle. Lift up your eyes to the hills. Lift up your voice in honor and worship to the King. Shout unto the Lord with a voice of triumph and bless Him. Right now bless His name!

Tell that problem how great your God is, and watch it come down. Enough is enough! You've got to press forward for the prize. Forgetting the things that are behind, let us reach ahead with new strength, stamina, and perseverance.

Declare to yourself "I must advance." I come into agreement with you and declare that you will advance, my brother, sister, daughter, and son. Though faced with extreme pressures, make Jesus your focus and pursue Him with all of your heart, mind, soul, and strength, for your life depends on it! With Him victory is imminent and without Him defeat is prominent.

Job declared, "Though he slay me yet will I trust Him." Extreme pressure brings extreme transformation. Job had been faithful to stand on God's promises. He chose not to worship material possessions or become distracted by the pressures that surrounded him. He focused to worship God alone.

Yes, he was overwhelmed by adversities. His faith and determination were even made a mockery. Yes, he sometimes complained of the adversities in spite of his right living. At times he even lost perspective. But he soon realized that life or how he feels do not dictate his outcome.

Your outcome, a breakthrough, victory, and triumph stem on one truth and that is God loves you. He will take care of you. In spite of the raging storm and calamities of life, we must be determined to trust God for victory, declare His promises and rest in His love. That's the relationship God is looking for. He is seeking someone who will be fully committed to His love. Job, Joshua, Jehoshaphat, Zerubbabel, Habakkuk, Israel, Paul, and Silas all stayed committed to worship and they received double favor, increase and empowerment to overcome every setback. They received victory on every side.

So grab hold of faith through the thresholds of worship and *push*. Don't you dare quit. Don't you dare throw in the towel! No matter what the weapon, storm, or adversity. No matter what the pressure or set back. You will win and be victorious. You are more than a conqueror. Never accept defeat but hold on and press through to victory. Press into His presence and see His glory fill your arena.

If you are facing sickness, a broken heart, a failed business, a failed marriage, or financial bondage, God says to you, "*Overcome!*" Expect the unexpected and experience the healing and victory He has for you today. Build your hope on the Lord Jesus Christ. When the rain comes down or the flood passes through, you will not be destroyed.

With an overwhelming flood, God will bring an end to your Nineveh, your place of struggle or adversity. You will stand on Christ the solid Rock. Even as Jehoshaphat received word from the Lord, there is a word for you today! Do not be afraid. Neither be dismayed. You will not have to fight this battle for the battle belongs to the Lord. Take up your position of faith. Take up your position of obedience. Take up your position of true worship. Pursue Christ and follow hard after Him. Again, your life depends on it. Break out in sincere worship to the King of Kings. Let Jesus be your everything, the Lover of your soul, all that your eyes behold.

We must engage through a heart-to-heart with God. We must stretch beyond the old boundaries of our own thinking and of those around us. Position yourself for the shift and wind of God that is blowing you into new territory. Leap into new heights as His wind blows you into supernatural realms of power, anointing, justice, breakthroughs, miracles, and supernatural provisions. God the righteous judge will render a final verdict on behalf of every injustice against His children. You will be fully restored and compensated. There is a shift and a deposit of God's Spirit being released. You will possess the land and inherit the Kingdom as you are positioned in relationship through worship.

> "As I watched, this horn was waging war against the saints and defeating them, until the Ancient of Days came and pronounced judgment in favor of the saints of the Most High, and the time came when they possessed the kingdom."
> —Daniel 7:21–22

It's pretty simple; if your bucket is empty you can never overflow. Through worship, the presence of the Lord will fill the cup of your soul over the brim, giving you the ability to overflow with His glory. You will overcome every struggle. You will overpower every enemy. You will overtake all that the Enemy has stolen. Let Jesus wrap you with all that He is. Experience healing and total victory. Expect victory, healing, and restoration on every side. Take up your position of faith, hope, and love. Stand firm in the confidence of the Almighty God that He is love and He will deliver! Draw nigh unto Him and He will draw nigh unto you. In the position of worship get "magnetized" and see His glory overtake you. You are not just a survivor. You are not just an overcomer—you are more than a conqueror! Receive it! Believe it! Expect it!

EXPECT THE UNEXPECTED

POSITION YOURSELF TO WORSHIP THE ALMIGHTY GOD!
EXPECT YOUR MIRACLE, EXPECT YOUR BREAKTHROUGH,
EXPECT YOUR HEALING, AND EXPECT YOUR DELIVERANCE!

A LIFE OF PRAYER AND CONSECRATION IS PREPARATION
FOR A DYNAMIC DEMONSTRATION
OF KINGDOM ADMINISTRATION

The Blessing of the Lord overtake you!

Prayer

You may have strayed away from the Father's love or you may have never had the invitation to receive Jesus as your Lord and Savior. Take a moment to say this prayer.

Father, I am a sinner and I am lost without You. Your Word declares that all have sinned and come short of Your glory. I realize that without You, my life and accomplishments are meaningless and empty. Today, I ask You to enter my heart and every arena of my life. Forgive me of all my sin, create in me a clean heart, and renew a right spirit within me. Today, You are the Lord of my life. I place You above all else and right now, I declare that I am a new creation. I am Your righteousness. I am more than a conqueror. Thank You, Jesus, for saving me! Thank You for setting me free!

ABOUT THE AUTHOR

DR. K.L. Bradwell is an anointed, apostolic, and prophetic vessel of God. She is a woman of much prayer, a worship powerhouse, and an anointed psalmist who maintains a passion to reap the end time harvest for her Lord. From her youth, she has maintained a hunger for His presence and He continues to be her pursuit. Her lifestyle of worship and prayer has kept her through many adversities, enabling her to reign and overcome. Having understood the dynamics of worship, she seizes every opportunity to encourage the body of Christ to run to the Father through the conduit of worship. She calls nations to pursue the presence of the Almighty God, to run after Him with reckless obedience, and to embrace His very heart. As a result, we are catapulted into a realm where His glory is unleashed into our arena, dismantling every power of darkness and liberating every captive soul. For in His presence there is fullness of Joy!

The mission field and life's challenges, testings, and trials have been her greatest teachers: placing within her a powerful ministry of worship, healing, and deliverance. She sets her eyes upon the Lord as the power of His Spirit transforms, eradicates, and releases an anointing to reign in the midst of every adversity. She has lived a powerful testimony of God's healing power and continues to experience His faithfulness and deliberate favor. Miraculously healed from multiple sclerosis, delivered from oppression, and transformed from various adversities, she stands victorious. Her unique testimony and approach of the Gospel reaches an expansive audience, proclaiming liberty to the oppressed, bringing hope and healing to weary hearts and restoration to wounded souls.

Repositioned and strategically positioned for such a time as this, she accepted the call and appointment to effectively serve and minister to the body of Christ. For over twenty-five years she has served the local church in multiple areas. She serves the pastoral ministry at her local church. She offers a wealth of knowledge in worship, church growth and development, evangelism and outreach and provides restorative counsel to victims and offenders of abuse, crisis, and trauma.

Through her unique presentation of the gospel and profound gifts of ministration, various opportunities of ministry are opened and as a result she

ABOUT THE AUTHOR

is a much sought after leader, preacher, teacher, and psalmist. The love of God within her, her boldness to believe, and her compassion to see others live as overcomers keep her steadfast in the Kingdom and enable her to flow through an anointing where supernatural healings and divine breakthroughs are released. Within her springs up a well of life that overflows with the presence of the Almighty God. Fulfilling her mandate and call, she boldly takes possession of every opportunity and encounter to share the love of God, win souls, and see lives transformed to the honor and glory of His Name. Pursuing Christ and advancing His Kingdom!

For ministry opportunities please contact
Dr. K.L. Bradwell at Spoken Word Ministries
404-451-6478.

Email Contact:
psalmistkb@aim.com

www.ingramcontent.com/pod-product-compliance
Lightning Source LLC
Chambersburg PA
CBHW030325080526
44584CB00012B/720